Crime and Punishment

Shantonu Sen explains why the CBI's hands are tied when it comes to nabbing the high and mighty

The Central Vigilance Commissioner's website displays a list, running into pages and pages, of bureaucrats facing corruption charges. This step, significant in ways more than one, has intrigued some, mystified others and of course, left many more sceptical. By identifying members of his fraternity and naming the allegedly corrupt, he obviously hopes to shame them and perhaps suggest that his reach will also extend to others if they are not careful. But his gesture alone hardly convinces anyone that the corrupt will really be indicted, investigated and imprisoned.

The first initiative to deal with corruption was the creation of the Delhi Special Police Establishment in 1943. Today, it is better known as the CBI. It may surprise many, but the CBI has no legal status. All efforts since the eighties to push the CBI Act through have floundered, thanks to the powerful lobby within the services and their political masters. The Delhi Special Police Establishment Ordinance, 1943, which was converted into an Act in 1947, continues to prop up the CBI.

Apart from Delhi, the CBI functions in all other states with their consent. Its role is limited, confined within the parameters of the consent notification. No employee of the state, and this includes members of the All India Services serving there, may be investigated by the CBI suo moto. However corrupt they may be they are all above the CBI. Those sent on deputation can be investigated. However, the corrupt rarely got selected for deputation. Some got in but there the politicians interfered.

In the late eighties, when the CBI wanted to probe some officials, Rajiv Gandhi and P Chidambaram inserted the proviso in the Single Directive, prohibiting a CBI probe, even a secret inquiry, without written clearance from the department secretary. Mr Vittal himself has been a secretary and probably has had to stop the CBI on its tracks on one or two occasions. Other secretaries believed in seeking one clarification after another. The offender soon became wise to the goings-on and suitably covered his tracks. The CBI found the subsequent investigation quite fruitless.

It learnt the lesson soon enough: that the effort that went into netting a 'decision-maker' in the government was not worth it. All the energy, time and passion spent in preparing the case for the secretary's approval went up in smoke. It decided to heed the advice of a CBI SP to his junior colleagues — to concentrate on probing the corrupt activities of the less fortunate members of the civil services and steer clear of the powerful. The CBI has got rid of this shackle only about a year ago.

But its shadow has not fully lifted. The CVC, whose creation in his present avatar, was part of the lifting of the prohibition, is still a trishanku. The Act which will really fortify them is still to be legislated. The states continue to lay down the ground rules before permitting the CBI to function there. Therefore, any optimism that it will now go all out against corrupt senior officials is premature.

This is also a different CBI from the one that earned kudos in the fifties and early sixties. Its team of hardworking and dedicated investi-gators had then secured the conviction of Shiv Bahadur Singh, a minister in erstwhile Rewa State, who was caught while accepting a bribe of Rs 25,000. It sent behind bars a former commerce secretary, a member of the elite Indian Civil Service. Central ministers and secretaries — K D Malivea, Harekrishna Mehtab, Biju Patnaik, TT Krishnamachari, H M Patel — and civil servants working in cahoots with them paid for their crimes as a result of a CBI probe. Dharma Teja, a shipping tycoon who enjoyed the patronage of the highest in the country, rotted in an Indian jail thanks to the CBI. A high court judge then said that he ranked CBI inquiries on a par with Supreme Court findings.

Today, the CBI is the object of mockery and ridicule — for botching the Jain 'Bandhu' bribery case, for failing to haul up the top civil servants in the urea scam and the Bofors scandal. To be fair, it has also earned some plaudits — for the Purulia Arms scandal and for getting General Vaidya's assassins hanged. However, going by its recent track record, there could be a grain of truth in the people's perception of the CBI as an agency vulnerable to political interference.

Adding names to the website will not improve matters. The nexus between corrupt civil servants and the crime syndicate that comprises most of today's politicians is deeply entrenched. What may budge them is a CBI Act and a CBI dedicated only to investigating the corrupt and reporting only to the CVC. Mr Vittal might want this, but more important, will he get it?
(Shantonu Sen is former joint director, CBI)

'Snap incestuous link between politicians, bureaucrats'

25/04/95

By S. Sen

The imperialist liked to call the civil service of India the steel frame. It sounded grand and imperious, with a touch of hauteur. In retrospect one wonders whether the British humour only meant to call it "steel collar" and used the word frame to satisfy the Indian sensitivity. The service was both a faithful Alsatian and a hateful blood hound, but it responded grandly and this steel frame became the most faithful ally of the British Raj. There were outstanding exceptions but most of the 'frame' suited the Raj admirably. It had just the right mailbip touch which responded to the hot pollee. It also had among its numbers, vicious elements which crushed all dissent. The Raj was delighted. It went about safely and systematically looting the country with the steel frame serving as the perfect buffer.

"No criticism is implied or meant. Duty was cast on the services and this duty was discharged. Mostly the frame acted within the rules and regulations, draconian in themselves, and only sometimes outside them. The excesses that took place were not always on instruction. More often than not individual perversity, and the desire to please, dictated the action. The same is true today. But the present steel frame, though rusting and breaking apart, is more pervasive and more massive. Whether in an imperialist Raj or in a democratic Raj, the Civil Service has been taught to act as a well trained dog, and does so.

But today's steel frame, unlike the one in the past, comprises a vast conglomerate, distinct and separate from each other in terms of background, education and upbringing. Each number is trained to respond to the command of the political masters who are present day inheritors of the Raj. Some of them, troubled by their oath to the constitution, act somewhat differently but these are a 'mad few'. The vast number of them has surrendered. This is not to denigrate the service but unfortunately, the truth is that there are too many black sheep.
The goals of the imperialist Raj and the goals of the Indian democratic Raj have rapidly coalesced. The steel frame, 50 years into a free India, finds it easier to swim with the tide. In fact, the civil service has changed its political masters. The corruption which flowered freely during the British Raj but which jolted almost to a stop under leaders of the freedom movement has come into its own since the late '60s. Safe in their high perch the leaders call fire their weapons from the shoulders of the civil service.

The civil service which was initially reluctantly plaint now enjoys a satisfactory partnership with those who have inherited the mantle of Robert Clive and Warren Hastings. In the late '60s the Civil Service, including the judiciary, was asked to adopt the philosophy of the government in power rather than look to the constitution of India. Since then the service has shrugged off their reluctance and become active abettors and earned grateful protection. Rewards too have been instantaneous — cushy promotions, postings, extensions, gubernatorial appointments, out of turn appointments, unimaginable clout and, of course, unimaginable lucre. This cosy relationship between the civil service and its political masters is to the advantage of both.

Mr T N Seshan talks about this. He is heard and is printed. Others, not heard, also talk about this protection. The people suffer it and endure it. Perhaps the only silver lining is that they will not do so for long. The time is not far off when public servants will be beaten up just because they are public servants. The attack will be brutal and will, as always, hurt most, the least concerned. The brutal killing of a Bihar IAS officer and the assassination of a Nagaland IAS officer in quick succession must not be dismissed only as unfortunate incidents. Those civil servants who are in nexus with organised crime syndicates that comprise most of the political masters today, may not be targeted initially but for how long? Sadly, no attempt has been made to change the frame. Most bureaucrats prefer to be ostriches.

But action is called for. We should shake off the dependence on government agencies to act against the corrupt and the criminal. A 93-year-old man in Tripura has thrown the gauntlet. A much younger maverick has done the same in the deep south. These efforts may be motivated but they have shown the way. The material they hire can only come from the civil service. The protective ring round the civil service needs easing.

Excessive secrecy which covers their decisions is not in public interest except in the rare instances of national security. We should abolish the official secrets Act or at least tone it down. Recruit young and legislate for their secure tenure. The public should be allowed to expose, prosecute and pillory the corrupt and the crime prone in the administration, both civil servants and their masters. Take away their protection. Snap that cosy, almost, incestuous relationship between the civil service and their democratically elected rulers.
(The writer is a joint director of the CBI)

The Tales Were Then Happening.

CBI
TALES FROM THE BIG EYE

SHANTONU SEN

Notion Press Media Pvt Ltd

No. 50, Chettiyar Agaram Main Road,
Vanagaram, Chennai, Tamil Nadu – 600 095

First Published by Notion Press 2021
Copyright © Shantonu Sen 2021
All Rights Reserved.

ISBN 978-1-68563-262-5

Dedicated to

Indraneil Chaudhuri, Amrita Dasgupta and Shubam Sen,

my three grandchildren, my first audience,

whom I engaged by telling a few of these tales

in much shorter formats.

Their remarkable interest, listening with their

mouths almost wide-open,

has persuaded me to tell these tales.

Contents

Foreword

Shri Shantonu Sen, the author of this book, has been a distinguished and respected senior officer of the CBI, who worked closely with me as Officer on Special Duty, looking after Police co-ordination and security matters during both my terms as Lt Governor, Delhi (1997-98; 2007-13) and provided most valuable support and assistance in respect of matters assigned to him.

I remember that during my first terms, on one of our Open Public Hearing Days at Raj Niwas, a simply clad lady came with her grievance that though her husband had been murdered, the Police had failed to investigate the case properly and had closed their file, thus denying her justice.

With my approval, Shri Sen called for the Case Diary from the Delhi Police, meticulously went through the record and noted that a very material line of investigation had not been pursued. He instructed the DCP (Crime Branch) to reopen the investigation. When this was done, the case was solved, the perpetrator of the crime charged, taken to Court and convicted after due judicial process.

Shri Sen's sharp intellect, honesty of purpose and professional determination to unravel the tangled threads in the serious cases assigned to him are evidenced in the cases recounted in this book. His two earlier books, A CBI Insider Speaks and CBI and Corruption, have cited many other notable cases where his investigative acumen, team leadership qualities and fearlessness appear in sharp relief.

Shri Sen retired as senior Joint Director in the CBI. I am certain that had destiny taken him to the post of Director, CBI, the organisation's reputation would have soared to that of a Fearless Eagle rather than what has been referred to as that of a "Caged Parrot".

New Delhi, August 27, 2021

Tejendra Khanna

Former Lt Governor,

Delhi

Preface

Nothing Slothful about this Sleuth

I met him in my avatar as a sleuth; with him trying to find out what I had found out!

It was 1992, the stock market and banking scam had just defrauded the investing Indian of around a billion dollars or more with enormous collateral damage to the Indian economy. The Indian Parliament was in a state of uproar. Unable to handle the heat, the government of the day, headed by Narasimha Rao, announced a JPC — a joint parliamentary committee — on the stock market to probe the irregularities in securities and banking transactions. It was only the second such JPC; the first having been the probe into the Bofors scandal. The intrepid Gurudas Dasgupta was amongst its members and hungry to get to the bottom of the scam. That was easier said than done.

As a journalist with the Statesman, I was snooping around for exclusive information as well and knew that all the documents seized during the raids were getting deposited in a big room in an annexe to the Parliament to which no one, save for the members of the JPC, had any access. Gurudas Babu was a friend and he requested the

Managing Director of the Statesman, C. R. Irani, if I could help him. CRI, always happy to go for a good story, agreed and thus I found myself in Delhi, under the pseudonym of Ms Krishna Roy, a low-key flunky with the CPI (to which Gurudas Babu belonged) but with access to the treasure trove of incriminating documents.

For me, it was like entering a huge vault filled with fat bundles of paper, without anyone having sorted out what was what. Like a little mouse, I pulled at one bundle a day, read the details and pieced the story together. The deal was that the story would be handed over to Gurudas Babu, who would then expose it at the JPC meet every evening. It was a trifle unsettling to see stories dug out by me being published by every reporter in the country, without any acknowledgment; but the experience made it worth its while.

It was one such day and I was busy typing up the story of the day at Gurudas Babu's one-roomed apartment at the Constitution Club of India, when I suddenly sensed that someone was standing right behind me. I looked back... then I looked up and up and up. There he was in a black 'galabandh', dark glasses, standing all of 10 feet — or so it seemed to my diminutive self — when he broke the silence, "I am Shantonu. I have come to see Mr Dasgupta". Gurudas Babu had not yet returned from Parliament and I offered his guest a seat. Little did I then know that he was the most dreaded man for stock market scamsters. Many other investigators had been compromised. Not Shantonu Sen.

That was the beginning of a friendship that has grown over the years. I have examined many cases that he has successfully handled and those that he has not. We have holidayed together, hosted expositions on creative excellence, dined in every exciting place in Kolkata and many in Delhi as our families became friends. Friendships are engendered by respect, common interests and shared values. We had all these going for us but possibly the most fascinating cement to this friendship has been Shantonu Sen's ability to tell a story over an 'adda'.

The word sleuth is derived from the Norse sloth that means to "trail" and Shantonu Sen had always insisted that trailing a lead meticulously, with an eye on minute details, following systems and processes, is what makes for a successful sleuth, who can win cases.

Not all his stories have been dramatic but all of them are replete with fascinating little details from his personal experiences that provide telling insights into the world of crime and its detection, his wordsmithy and the delectable twists in the tales, even if they end in the disappointment of having good work trashed by processes in an imperfect system.

Tales From the Big Eye presents a dozen more plus three.

Aditi Roy Ghatak

Author's Note

Experiences over my career have convinced me that sometimes the more audacious manage to get away with crime in this country. They have the ability to 'persuade' people who should book them to 'root' for them.

I have had the befuddling experience of a Chief Justice of the Bombay High Court being in the pay of an Indian drug lord for years without any one being the wiser for it. When exposed, another Supreme Court judgement — erring on both legal and factual grounds — helped him to escape exemplary punishment. All that he got was a rap on the wrist. He quit without a blemish on his record and went on to teach budding lawyers at the National Law College, Kolkata.

Yet again, two Supreme Court Judges ensured the liberty of established felons on grounds that went against the law and facts. Those spared included a Minister, his secretary, and a corporate (company), even though the CBI investigations and their trial in the anti-terrorist court had found them guilty of a heinous crime and sentenced them to undergo rigorous imprisonment for several years and pay substantial fines as well.

The real tragedy is that only the foot soldiers pay. In the 1993 blasts, the brains in Pakistan and the arch criminal, Dawood Ibrahim, remained way beyond reach. His co-conspirator and brother, Anees, was caught in Bahrain on our Interpol alert. We were asked by Interpol Bahrain to fetch him. We went. He was then whisked away from under our very noses thanks to the influence wielded by his brother, Dawood Ibrahim.

After his arrest in Bahrain, the United Arab Emirates (UAE) discovered that he was wanted for a crime. They put forward their claim and, being an Arab state, they got priority. Yet, he was never tried in the UAE. It was a ruse and our government was indifferent. The power of the top criminal, a don, a judge or a politician is enormous. My books and stories have reflected on the use and misuse of such powers.

There are also stories of good detection. Give your time to the investigation, think about it and be patient, relying on your findings. Crime is inevitable and no criminal is invincible. Yes, courts may not always agree but an honest detection is indifferent to the court's indifference.

I have tried to put together an account of my experiences for the layman to understand how the arm of the law works and why it fails to work at times. I do hope many more in the field of criminal justice system will tell their tales. It will enhance knowledge about this much derided system and, in the process, introduce measures that might help improve it. My earlier accounts have been published by Manas

Publishers, 2015: CBI INSIDER SPEAKS and Authors Upfront, 2020: CBI, CORRUPTION AND I. They have been well received. That has encouraged me to write another fifteen here.

Shantonu Sen

Being a Detective

I was hoping to be pushing files after qualifying in the Union Public Service Commission, expecting to be a bureaucrat — a *babu* — when the government of India decided that I should be a detective. I had no choice in the matter. I was told to be a detective and I became one with lots of gusto and gumption and no training. In 1963, detective training in India, meant outdoor exercises, weapons training, reading criminal acts, the Indian Penal Code, Criminal Procedure Code, Indian Evidence Act and learning to march in step, salute smartly and learn to obey.

Asking questions? I did not see much of that. So when I was, sort of, thrown into the deep end, I sank. I drank what sucked me in, I retched and threw up. Since I did not drown, I repeated it quite often till I learnt to float. This took the better part of two years, 1965 to 1967, before I became a detective of sorts. The first taste of success, which came after many a stumble and several failures, is still fresh in my mind, though it happened way back in late 1965, when I was still sinking. The person under investigation was a Deputy Director ranked officer in the Ministry of Commerce, working from Calcutta.

I was still a probationer having completed the course and field training. The task before me was to find his wealth that was hidden from most eyes. I had failed in the first few attempts in such cases. Smarter from my earlier experiences, where I had floundered, I tried a different tack in this case. First, I reduced the period of check to seven years only and followed the money trail through his bank deposits and withdrawals. Normally, the period of check to detect assets disproportionate to known sources of income covers the entire service period of the one being investigated. I selected a limited period and then picked and documented his payments such as children's school fees, electricity, gas bills, house rent, purchases of petrol, payment for his monthly rations, grocery bills and others.

By sticking to a smaller check period, what I remember at this distance is, I was able to show that, in that limited period, he had an unaccountable wealth of ₹24,000 and odd. That was a considerable sum of disproportionate wealth in 1966. This charge stuck to him and the person who was Deputy Director in the office of Director General of Supplies and Disposals Calcutta, was tried departmentally. I attended the departmental enquiries and, in the face of strenuous steps to derail the investigation, stood by the charge of the unexplained income. My strategy of going for a narrower period to scrutinise expenses as opposed to the entire career was disputed vigorously. I overcame all the arguments and he was removed from service. That was my first break as a detective in the CBI in Calcutta.

The next was a biggie. It was in Delhi and it was a matter of some importance. The year was 1967. The CBI then had, and still has, investigating units like Police Stations with the difference. The Station House Officers (SHO) in the CBI are ranked as Superintendent and Investigation Officers are Deputy Superintendents and Inspectors. Other ranks, those of a Sub Inspector, Assistant Sub Inspectors, Head Constable, Constables, only assist them. They do not independently investigate. My unit was named Fraud Squad I.

The entire unit had a team of four Deputies, eight Inspectors, with a host of members from other ranks. I was the sole UPSC recruited direct Deputy Superintendent. I was investigating independently as were the other three. We were all groping to uncover how a group of textile mills under the umbrella of the G. D. Birla textile empire, was evading excise duties and if the manner of doing it was a crime. It was only after studying their correspondence with the Ministry of Textile officers and Textile Commissioner that I was able to figure out their *modus operandi.*

The mills were paying excise on an item as 'coarse' cloth, though in terms of its quality — determined by its reed and pick — it should have been defined as 'fine' cloth in accordance with the Textile Commissioner's notifications, issued from time to time, on what was super fine, fine and coarse. The excise is accordingly notified in government notifications and textile mills self-assess and pay excise duties accordingly. Curiously, all Birla textile mills under investigation were, at that point of time, writing to the Textile Commissioner in unison to change the existing definition of 'coarse' to fit in with what they were doing, paying lower excise, as determined for coarse cloth, even on fine cloth.

The correspondence carried on for months. The excise evasion also continued. They ceased when they were rejected for the third or fourth time. The charge was how the textile that was essentially superior was declared 'coarse' for excise purposes, to pay an infinitely smaller amount as excise. Sizeable amounts were then creamed off as profits from sales. Their lawyers were the best, Ashoke Sen, Hira Lal Sibal and others, who got the CBI to stop searches, got trial courts to see this as no crime but only a difference of opinion. However, the charge of evasion of excise stuck against the textile mills and other mills. Lakhs evaded in excise was recoverable.

Then came the exciting experience of 1968. Indira Gandhi's signature was traced and then forged by the cheat and an attempt was made to cheat K. M. George, Managing Director, Bokaro Steel Plant. The scam was to forge the Prime Minister's signature, get Mr George to accept it as genuine and act upon it. The cheat nearly succeeded. However, Mr George checked with the PMO and that is how the investigation began. The cheat had left his name and address. Picking him up from his address was an option. I carefully considered it but dropped the idea. The address could be only a place for correspondence. Then it would only reach me to an accomplice, who could well be not privy to it all. The cheat and forger could be two different persons.

To my mind, the attempt to get them all in one fell swoop would be a risk but one well worth taking. I wanted to inveigle him to the scene of his crime; entice, seduce and entrap. Let him be tempted by a belief that there was more in the offing. The evidence in court that he himself was the author of the traced forgery was thereby much the easier to prove. The entrapment required drama, actors — some of the plant employees were given defined roles — and patience. After laying the trap it proved to be a long wait; a full seven days. In fact, cooling my heels in Bokaro hoping and praying that the culprit would walk in was an exercise in patience.

Well, he did. Ram Surat Rai was caught with his tools and accessories! These included forged letter heads of other Union Ministers as well. He was travelling on a forged railway pass and he had readymade passes for future use. With this entrapment and more, his trial and conviction in several more similar crimes was possible. His crimes covered Bihar and Uttar Pradesh. He was tried both in Patna and Lucknow and both courts sent him behind bars for years of incarceration.

By now my nose had got trained and I could sniff things out better. Later, again in 1968, my detective skills were tested further. The story in brief was that the State

Trading Corporation (STC) Delhi, while balancing its accounts in the SBI, Delhi, had a shortfall of ₹48,000. The probe revealed two cheques, issued four months apart by its Protocol Cell for ₹10 and ₹38 each, had caused a debit of ₹48,000. This ₹48,000 was fraudulently obtained as the claims themselves were false. Deeper probe established that the STC cheques of ₹10 and ₹38 were debited for much higher amounts: ₹10 for ₹10,000 and ₹38 for ₹38,000; ₹48,000 was a phenomenal amount for the STC in 1968.

Though the CBI, Delhi Branch, had received the complaint, there was no result even after four months and the STC top brass was blowing its top. Mr Prakash Tandon, the then Chairman, was a corporate icon. He was both powerful and imperious enough to read the riot act to F. V. Arul of the I. P. (Imperial Police) then Director, CBI. A very annoyed Director flayed the Delhi Branch Chief, a Deputy Inspector General and, to add insult to injury, transferred the investigation to Fraud Squad I, CBI. That brought me in. My unit head was N. R. Suvarna. He was seasoned, helpful and encouraged me to think out of the box.

It was a white collar crime. There were documents to scrutinise. I was looking for a verifiable address. I looked for them in the applications made for opening the two current accounts. Both had addresses. The current account operated from Allahabad Bank, Hauz Quazi Branch, where ₹10,000 was credited, had a verifiable address. In the other bank, where ₹38,000 was credited, the address was fake. Opening an account, savings or current, required neither photograph, PAN card nor an Aadhar Card in those days.

The verifiable address had nearly 40 people occupying it! One conclusion that I had reached and was sanguine about was that the forger and cheat was an STC employee, who had pulled off the heist. I recall 52 years to the day that I directed ASI Ram Singh, on deputation from Delhi Police to the CBI/Fraud Squad I, to locate the STC employee among the residents. I was hugely disappointed when after three days he sent a negative report. I was still convinced that my detective senses were right. I assigned the same work to Head Constable Narendra Singh Chawla, a CBI officer. I briefed him as well as possible. To my great delight he returned with a confirmation. He had taken a week working on his investigation. He located the STC employee and identified him.

Chawla had also obtained data on the desk (Protocol Cell) that he occupied at STC. That was excellent work and with that data, I nabbed the criminal with enough material to put him in the lock-up for 14 days. In weeks I had solved the crime. I was cock-a-hoop, Suvarna was delighted and F. V. Arul was relieved. Ramesh Chand Sharma was convicted in both cases of fraud and forgery. There was plenty by way of investigation still to do before he was finally jailed. All that was completed in due course.

By 1970, five years of slogging and 'detective work', under the excellent guidance from N. R. Suvarna of the Indian Police Service, Tamil Nadu Cadre, S.P. and Chief Investigating Officer of the Fraud Squad I, helped me brush off the novice tag. In the last two years, when the novice tag — the sobriquet the direct recruits are given by veteran detectives — was no longer a refrain, I looked forward to my promotion. Before that it was once more into the hustings. N. R. Suvarna chose to throw me a gauntlet. This one was different.

A veteran deputy superintendent had spent six months investigating a case and his advice was that there was nothing criminal in the allegations. The case featured the Oil and Natural Gas Commission (ONGC). Suvarna did not agree. He directed a reinvestigation. The charge arose out of an internal audit paragraph of a conscientious auditor of the Oil and Natural Gas Commission Eastern Oil Field (ONGC ER), one P. K. Dey. It objected to the Chairman ONGC, approving a total payment of ₹27 lakhs by ONGC ER, by splitting the payments that arose out of one agreement between ONGC ER and the management of Lukwah Tea Estate (LTE) into several orders.

The auditor was of the opinion that this was done to avoid sending the proposal to the government of India and a financial impropriety had thus been committed. Mr L. J. Johnson of the Indian Civil Service (ICS) as Chairman, ONGC, examined the audit para sitting with the Board of ONGC and overruled it on the ground this para ignored the requirement of 'higher audit', which should have considered propriety and commercial considerations of the ONGC ER as primary and not just the rules of audit.

The Board saw this objection as red tape and dropped it. However, fate intervened. LTE Sibsagar was the property of then Treasurer, Congress Party. The Opposition in Parliament got wind of it. A short notice question debate followed. The upshot was the government conceding to a CBI investigation. My predecessor, Ved Prakash, also saw no merit in the audit para for the same reasons. His superior and mine, N. R. Suvarna, did not agree and that is how I got the authority to review this investigation.

The audit para had been raised a year ago. I knew little of tea garden functioning and even less of tea plantations. I had to take a crash course in both. Assam in 1970 was land's end. Ved Prakash had done all his enquiries in Delhi. He was in his fifties while I was in my 29th year. I was determined to take the course in Assam. I visited a couple of tea gardens, Hathikola Tea Gardens nestling Kaziranga, is a vivid memory. An Englishman was the manager there. He was hospitable and helpful. He took me through the office and factory and then through the books and records that most tea gardens customarily maintained and operated. That long evening with a blazing fireplace, scotch and going over and over the books, followed by early dinner with the host are still a memory. The next morning, he organised a trip inside Kaziranga Forest Reserve in the tea garden's specially fitted jeep!

Thus armed and knowledgeable, I approached the court with a list of LTE internal records that I wanted to study. They were to be obtained from its factory, its offices in Sibsagar and its registered headquarters at Calcutta. I obtained a search warrant for all three. The searches were conducted simultaneously. The records were in the hundreds. The next step was to study them, understand them and to know how the contents related to what is to be investigated.

That was my job. In the business of investigation, understanding of the case must follow this process. Later, the author of the document can be interviewed. I took notes for six months. Then I questioned the authors travelling to and fro between Sibsagar, Calcutta and the ONGC Headquarters at Dehra Dun from Delhi. Patience and arduous work finally revealed the contours of the suspicious action to me. The audit para was the starting point. The amount of ₹27 lakhs was suspicious. It should have been less, substantially so.

The agreement between the ONGC ER and LTE Sibsagar stipulated compensation for 300 *bighas* at about ₹3 lakhs. The balance ₹24 lakhs paid was for tea bushes on the 300 *bighas* of land. It was, if I remember correctly, ₹11 for each tea-bearing bush. Any bush more than 12-15 years old or less than three years old was not tea bearing and hence no compensation would be paid, as specifically stipulated in the agreement.

LTE stood on 12 acres of land and the going rate for the tea garden, in 1970, was about ₹12 lakhs. Paying ₹23 lakhs for tea-growing bushes on 300 *bighas*, I knew, deep down, was foul play. The crime, if any, lay here. I probed deeper. In an LTE tea garden, tea was planted either in triangular or rectangular patterns. The 10 blocks, comprising 300 *bighas* acquired for oil drilling by ONGC ER within the LTE, were so planted.

The bushes were shown in thousands. Were they separately counted? The answer was no. The area acquired and the plantation method that was practiced were put together to arrive at the total number of bushes, I found. When I inspected the other sections of plantation, I found vacant areas, indicating that bushes had died. Bushes do die. I was quite sure that by not physically counting each bush, payment had been made for non-existing bushes.

It stood to reason that in the acquired areas too, a number of bushes would be dead and missing. So ONGC ER could have paid for tea bushes that were not there, I surmised. More serious was that small print in the agreement. It was agreed that tea bushes less than three years and more than 12-15 years old would get no compensation because they did not supply tea. Deeper probe revealed that LTE always planted and replanted one section in the garden in the same year.

The 300 *bighas* acquired by ONGC ER were a part of those weeded and re-planted sections. My learning process had primed me to the fact that tea gardens maintained meticulous records of planting, re-planting and removal of non tea-bearing tea bushes. Why? Because the Tea Board of India inspects them, relies on them and pays handsome subsidies for uprooting the non tea-producing bushes and planting seedlings.

Just after receiving the bulk of compensation from ONGC ER, LTE Sibsagar had claimed and obtained this subsidy for removing non tea-growing bushes from the same sections. To emphasise the point, tea bushes are planted in the same year in the same section. This was done here, I was confident. I investigated accordingly. This investigation opened a can of worms. Almost 90 per cent of the acquired land had non tea-bearing bushes!

This was proved both by the LTE Sibsagar records and the record of subsidy maintained by the Tea Board of India. After more than a year I had my findings. A horrendous crime had been perpetrated. I had a lot more work to do to seriously tighten the screws. In criminal investigations, the role of each criminal; his or her role in perpetrating the crime, all needed solid work to detect but the tunnel was ending. However, man proposes and God disposes.

In late-1971, I received my promotion orders. From being No. 5 in my batch of seven, I was catapulted to No. 2 by the Selection Committee. Also, only three out of seven were promoted and I alone, of the three, received independent charge. I handed over the remaining investigations to Inspector M. D. Singh, who was my deputy in this case and I moved to Calcutta as Superintendent, Economic Offences Wing in early January 1972. In mid-1976, I was moved up as Superintendent I (One) CBI, General Offences Wing, Calcutta.

In June 1979, I was promoted as Deputy Inspector General (outside the cadre), Sikkim Vigilance Police with the government of Sikkim at Gangtok. For 11 years I hardly did any direct detective work. A number of skilled, semi-skilled and, occasionally, utterly raw detectives reported to me. My job was to ensure they did not get derailed. My mentors were primarily two. A. B. Chaudhury, who initially taught me CBI work and then N. R. Suvarna who, in Fraud Squad I, Delhi, imparted comprehensive detective skills.

There were prosecutors reporting to me as well. I supervised their court work. I did no detectiving. That was not to be till 1983, when I returned to Delhi. These 11 years have been rich in experience and with varied lessons learnt, which I hope to recount some time. At the end of my three-year tenure in Sikkim, I returned to being a detective again. I had to forfeit the advantage of a higher rank in Sikkim as it was outside the CBI.

It was not till 1985 that I earned the next rank in CBI, that of a Deputy Inspector General.

The Typewriter Expert

October 1982; Krishan Sikand, 39 years of age, found himself in love for the second time. His first marriage had ended in a divorce. His new love, Rani Chowdhury, was a widow of an Airforce officer, killed in action in 1971. She was married again in 1976 but very unhappily so. By 1982, she wanted out. She loved Krishan Sikand and they lived together at his place in 98, Sunder Nagar. Their bedroom was on the first floor.

Krishan Sikand's son from his first marriage, around 11, was celebrating a relative's birthday party on the lawns of the Sunder Nagar apartment on 2nd October, 1982. It was evening. He wanted his father to come down and join the celebrations. Krishan was alone in his room. Rani had driven off that morning to Sanawar, where her both daughters, from her first marriage, studied. The boy decided to invite his father to the lawns and took some snacks on a plate, wafted up the stairs, and knocked timidly on his daddy's bedroom door.

His father did not like to be interrupted at work. Asked to enter, he did and after giving his father the plate of food asked him to come down. Krishan, taciturn as ever, nodded and the son scampered back to the lawns. A while back, a family retainer had taken a letter-cum-parcel addressed to Krishan, that had been half stuffed into the letter box, which was accessible to all and sundry, up to his room. Ten or 12 minutes after the boy left the room, there was a loud blast in Krishan's room. Krishan died in the blast and the Delhi Police took up the investigation.

After five months of no detection, the Delhi Police was ordered by the Ministry of Home Affairs to transfer the investigation to the CBI. Thus, this case of unnatural death of Krishan Sikand became the baby of a Central Investigation Unit of the CBI. I was the Superintendent of that investigation unit and took charge of the investigation on 19th March, 1983. My first job was to visit the scene of crime but where was the scene of crime? The room had been repaired and was under use. The post-blast debris was packed in two large suitcases by the Delhi police and their custodian at that time was the Central Forensic Laboratory (CFSL), R. K. Puram. Its ballistic expert was Dr G. R. Prasad. So it was there that we, the investigating officer and I, set forth. We spent a total of nine hours over two days with Dr Prasad.

What did we unearth? We certainly found out how Krishan Sikand was killed. We found the booby trap that had blasted him to pieces. It was a service hand grenade. We established from the pieces collected from the scene of crime that this hand grenade was made in a Pakistan Ordnance factory. The debris threw up much more valuable feedback. We found it was fired with an igniter/detonator manufactured in the Kirkee, Pune Ammunition Factory, in 1964. We also found that the hand grenade had been put inside a tubular box, which was used to pack badminton shuttlecocks. M/s Artex Industries, Bombay, used these boxes, we later found.

This particular box, just like other similar boxes, had a white plastic lid at each end. This box had been cut to a size making it possible to place the hand grenade inside expertly with the help of a twisted copper wire, which was also found at the scene of crime. This was released as soon as the pressure of the packing material eased. This is what happened as soon as Krishan Sikand opened the parcel. Death was instantaneous and horrible. The entire body was disfigured and burnt. The haemorrhage and the shock bled the vital organs, with heart and lung stopping, kidneys bleeding and the brain dying.

Apart from the clues from the debris, which was material telling us how Krishan Sikand died, we also picked bits and pieces from the debris that helped us greatly to find the killer.

- We found the scattered pieces of paper that, when pieced together, gave us the typed address of Krishan Sikand on the parcel containing the killer hand grenade. The man had been blasted to bits but, remarkably, the pieces of the parcel had survived. Finding all the torn pieces and placing them together to make it all readable was the red letter moment of the investigation.

- On the addressee's side it read 'Krishan Sikand,

98, Sunder Nagar, Delhi' and on the sender's side it read Delhi Metals, 200 Hauz Quazi, Delhi 110006. That this was a fake address was soon established.

- We also collected from the ashes within the debris a strong red thread, which proved to be a valuable lead much later during the investigation.

With this material, we set out to get to the bottom of the murder. Many discussions took place among the team of sleuths that was set up to find clues and the perpetrators. We were aware of Dr Edmond Locard's Exchange Principle stating that whenever two objects come in contact, there is some transfer of material. We had some objects sent by the killers, which caused Krishan Sikand's death. Who sent them? We had now that difficult task, where the Delhi Police had floundered.

Murder has a motive. We worked on this hard and long. We found out that Rani's former and now estranged husband, one Lt Col S. J. Chaudhary, aka Jeeti, was terribly upset with Krishan and Rani for living together before the divorce between them was final. He had been threatening them with harm, including death. A very distraught Rani, shattered by Krishan's grisly end — but for sheer providence she would have been included too — narrated his threats to us. We checked and found this to be true.

The murder modus operandi clearly pointed to a military operation. We bit the bullet. Zeroing on him as our only suspect, one early morning we swooped upon all the addresses where he had links. His own address in Pragati Vihar Hostel, where he occupied a suite, his mother's house in Friend's Colony where he occasionally stayed, his office in Vayu Bhawan as well as his personal car, a Standard Herald.

What were we looking for? Links. With what our nine hours of combing the debris had thrown up and what we found on this trail, we did. We found a wire cutter from his Herald and red-coloured string pieces, identical to the thread from the debris, from his office drawer. We were desperately looking for a typewriter. That we did not find. We were now keen to subject him to questioning; to grill him; to take him into custody and get our hands on him.

There was a big but. He was Lt Col S. J. Chaudhary, a serving Armed Corp Officer. He was a Sword of Honour cadet and a Veer Chakra holder! His father, the late S. R. Chaudhary, was a Punjab Cadre Indian Police Service officer, who had retired as Inspector General of the Delhi Police. His mother was socially prominent and was a frequent visitor to 7, Race Course Road, the Prime Minister's official residence. However, we had a murder case to solve.

I ordered his arrest as custodial interrogation was imperative. In 1983, the CBI was not interfered with but there were pressures following his arrest. Queries flowed again and again asking me to justify the arrest. There were repeated calls to justify the arrests and the CBI Director, J. S. Bawa, who was a Punjab Cadre Indian Police Service officer, handed most of them to me. I had to respond adequately. There were some telephone calls, which were not to my liking but the die was cast. Questions continued to flow.

Such a senior officer! Had I thought out all the consequences of an arrest almost 10 months after the crime? Would the court sustain the arrest? He was on an important desk and his arrest would interrupt his work in his office. Did I not know that he was also an international golf umpire and his arrest would become an issue if he was not available for umpiring abroad after committing himself? Had I anticipated these consequences?

I may or may not have but I answered them and, having arrested the suspect, went ahead with the interrogation. We had 24 hours initially. Three teams of officers took up the questioning. They succeeded in pinning him down.

He broke down and admitted that he could not tolerate Rani, his yet-to-be divorced wife, living 'in sin' with Krishan. It was then time to seek more time from the court. Chaudhary was arrested on Ist August, 1983. The court was given enough grounds to believe that he was the most likely suspect and we had many areas to question him on. We needed more time. Despite stiff opposition from the defence, we were given time till

8th August, 1983 to question him. Our main focus was to link him with the parcel that booby-trapped Krishan.

Who had typed the addresses on the parcel? The entire scheme of questioning centred here. Had Chaudhary done it? Had he organised it? He denied, denied and stuck to his denial. We persisted because in his persistent denials we saw and felt that he was hiding and hoping that we would stop this line of questioning. So there were bouts of questioning in other areas, when he was relaxed and confident and then back to the typed addresses on the fatal parcel.

Finally, he broke down and admitted that the address on the parcel, which was booby trapped to kill Krishan and Rani, was typed at the Janta Commercial College, I-43, Lajpat Nagar-II, New Delhi. In front of witnesses, he stood in custody and identified the premises. It was a shop that taught aspiring typists to learn typing. This was that era when communications were typed, signed and either hand delivered or posted. The era of mails and internet was yet to arrive.

We were on this scene in the first week of August 1983 and the crime had taken place on 2nd October, 1982, almost 10 months ago. There were 12 typewriters in the shop in 1983. Were they all there in September-October 1982? We had to prove that beyond doubt. We did. There was more. Most of these typewriters receive rough treatments and many letters get disfigured. They are then replaced. Which are those? That too was found out.

Fortunately, the most vital typewriter remained virtually unchanged; only two alphabets were disfigured and the keys had to be replaced. Locating the exact typewriter that typed the addresses on the all-too important parcel was a breakthrough. The expert established this with the help of admitted typed documents on this typewriter that were available for the period when the accused had visited the college to get his work done in the last week of September, 1982 and specimen typed material taken during investigation.

To do that accurately and also get the court to believe it, it was vital to have typed sheets from the suspected typewriter taken contemporaneously. Once the typewriter was identified, we rummaged through the shop if we could find some such sheets. We could do so as it was a teaching place and maintained records, student wise and typewriter wise, for one year at least. To our good luck, such sheets with the name of the person who had typed it and the date on which he had typed it were found.

The handwriting expert, S. K. Gupta of CFSL, Delhi, took up the job of forensically identifying the typewriter used by the college to have the address given by Chaudhary typed. He did so only after he was satisfied that we, as investigators of a murder case, had given him enough specimen and admitted material to compare with the questioned material, which in this case was the all too important addresses on the killer parcel. He explained this in his written opinion and the trial court accepted his opinion. In this process the confession of Chaudhary before the CBI would also be corroborated. His detailed reasoning confirming the use of the typewriter was an important pillar for nailing Chaudhary. There was more.

- The wire cutter recovered from his Herald was sent to the Indian Institute of Science, Bangalore, along with copper wire recovered from the scene of crime (found by us in the debris) to match the striations on the copper wire with edges of the cutter. Thus we had confirmation there as well.

- The red thread found in his office drawer was also proven to match the similar coloured red thread found in the debris.

The CBI has a tier system of examining the evidence collected. M. P. Singh, the investigating officer wrote his finding first and, after justifying that the evidence collected warranted Chaudhary's prosecution, he recommended his prosecution for both murder and use of explosive substances. My legal adviser did the same thereafter. When it came to me I wrote:

"The entire evidence is circumstantial. But this evidence is an inextricable net comprising evidence of motive, of threat, of dexterity, of involvement, of conduct and it is tightly laced with the evidence of experts."

My immediate boss, the Deputy Inspector General, then looked into the evidence along with his legal advisor. Both fully backed our findings. The Special Inspector General, who is also Joint Director, CBI and Director, CBI and the Legal Advisor, CBI found no reason to disagree either. Chaudhary who remained in judicial custody all through this exercise was sent to trial in November 1983. He faced charges of murder and use of explosive substances. However, the trial was halted when the sheet anchor of our entire evidence, the expert opinion of the typewriter expert, S. K. Gupta, was made unacceptable. This was not unexpected.

The Indian Supreme Court with three justices sitting together had in the Nirgudkar vs State of Madhya Pradesh AIR 1952 SC page 343, in an *obiter dicta* said: "typewriter experts evidence cannot be brought on record and be evaluated by the court." Since then American and English Courts had ruled otherwise. It was 1983 and both S. K. Gupta and I were confident that when this opinion was seen, the larger bench would reverse the 1952 one line *obiter*.

Unfortunately, we could not file an appeal before a five-bench Supreme Court straightaway. The process was prolonged. It took 13 years before our appeal could come up before a five-judge Constitutional Bench of the Supreme Court. This bench heard what was really an appeal against the one line *obiter* of three judges of a 1952 bench of the Supreme Court. After hearing us and the defence, Justice J. S. Verma, as he was then, pronounced, on behalf of his brother Judges, on 13th February, 1996:

"The examination of the typewriting and identification of the typewriter on which the questioned document was typed is based on a scientific study of certain significant features and its individualities, which can be studied by experts having professional skills on the subject, Therefore, his opinion on that point relates to an expert in the field of science (and) falls within the ambit of Section 45 of the Indian Evidence Act."

The trial Court, relying on the expert evidence, convicted Chaudhary holding him guilty of murder and use of explosive substances. He was sentenced to undergo life imprisonment. What is important is that after 40 years — from 1952 to 1996 — the country got a new expert, the Typewriter Expert.

Did it mean the end of the story though, even 13 years after the incident? It was clear even during the trial stage that the accused would not give up easily. He was a man with tremendous influence. The case was keenly contested at each step in the trial court. On 3rd May, 2008, the judge, a lady, read out her judgement, convicting Lt Col S. J. Chaudhary, aka Jeeti, who had retired by then, under both the Explosive Substances Act and murder, sentencing him to life.

Lt Col S. J. Chaudhary (Retired) was then 71 years old and the complainant, Sanjay Sikand, who was around 11 years old on 2nd October, 1982, was then 37 years of age. He consoled himself at last that he had achieved closure on the death of his ill-fated father. The judge had a word of praise for the investigation and wrote that there was no link connecting the murderer with the crime that had escaped investigation. The links pointed to the hand of the accused and only this accused, the judge concluded.

This investigation, immediately, became a staple book for teaching CBI probationary officers circumstantial evidence. However, Chaudhary appealed before the Delhi High Court. Ram Jethmalani along with others defended him and within a year, on May 15, 2009, a single judge of the Delhi High Court rejected S. K. Gupta's expert opinion on the typewriter on certain technicalities[1]. The Typewriter Expert was a reality though, a 5-Bench Supreme Court Constitutional Bench had said so.

In this case, the Judge's order said that "it is unfortunate that a crime is going unpunished" but its judicial conscience was not satisfied that the evidence conclusively established the guilt of the person charged. The Supreme Court maintained the acquittal. The entire judgement makes for compelling reading for the obvious questions that remain unanswered.

The 2009 Delhi High Court judgement of Mr Justice P. Nandrajog, then a recently elevated judge from the Delhi bar, set aside the conviction of the accused.

---

1   *https://www.casemine.com/judgement/in/56090cd6e4b014971117826e*, *https://indiankanoon.org/doc/292672/*, State thro CBI New Delhi Vs SJ Choudhary AIR 1996 SC 1491 Evidence Act Scientific/Expert Evidence,   *http://tnsja.tn.gov.in/article/SC%20Judgments%20Index.pdf*, https://indiankanoon.org/doc/894244/

His was a long judgement. The main grounds and the counterpoints tell a great deal about how the law works occasionally:

1. The Defence Witnesses had not been given weight but dismissed as interested witnesses by the trial court. His Lordship chose to overlook the trial judge's weighty reasons for not accepting the accounts of those witnesses.

2. There were three letters by the accused, the last in March 1982, showing that he was trying to reconcile desperately. In March 1982, he was reconciled to the separation and divorce. His Lordship trashed the trial judge for not highlighting this but ignored the evidence of more than half a dozen prosecution witnesses, who faced cross examination and narrated repeated stories of threats following quarrels between the two, which continued way beyond March 1982. Incidentally, the writer of these letters did not depose and, obviously, was not cross examined. The trial court could not take evidentiary notice and rightly so. His Lordship also should have done the same.

3. His Lordship dismissed the eye witness evidence of Shaif Ali who saw the accused lurking in the evening around 98, Sunder Nagar around the time the parcel bomb was delivered to this address only because the witness was an employee of Sikand Motors, implying that an employee would come to his employer aid; no questions asked!

4.   His Lordship has written a treatise on expert evidence on typewriters. The only aim was to show that S. K. Gupta, an MSc in chemistry, was no expert and only the two private experts who came as defence witnesses were believable. The trial court had held the opposite view and gave reasons that were more than adequate.

5.   The owner of the Janta Commercial College, P. W. Sethi, giving his evidence, remembered that the addresses were typed at the instance of the person who brought the addresses on a slip of a paper, though he could not identify the person who got it done. The trial court had assessed his deposition and cross, seen him in person, studied his demeanour and believed him. However, his Lordship, without the benefit of hearing him, trashed him by saying he had just gone along with the CBI officers! It would be pertinent to ask how he came to this conclusion and also wonder if there was a predetermination to quash the trial court's views.

6.   On the use of a hand grenade from the Pakistan Ordnance Factory, while the prosecution gave enough evidence of the accused having both opportunity and time to keep one as a trophy, His Lordship, without any evidence of such hand grenades being available, stated that 1982 was the peak of terrorism and hence such hand grenades were freely available! These were both unfounded positions and taken without a shred of evidence, beyond word play.

7. On the question of motive, His Lordship did not have it in him to dismiss it but went on to dismiss it as saying that motive alone was not enough. In the process, he trashed the motive, heavily supported with prosecution evidence. Yet the motive was adequately established for the accused to be indicted by the trial court.

Thus his Lordship acquitted the trial court murderer by accepting the evidence of the Defence Witnesses, by rejecting the evidence of S. K. Gupta, the expert from the CFLS; by trashing the eye witness, who saw the accused when he delivered the fatal parcel; and by mocking P. W. Sethi, owner of the Janta Commercial College, suggesting that his evidence about the addresses on the parcel being typed at his college was a statement made to please CBI officers.

It may be emphasised that the Janta Commercial College was identified by the accused himself! Admittedly, he did it while in police custody. Some may wonder how the confession of an accused against himself made to the police is evidence. It is because he did so under the relevant provision of the Indian Evidence Act (section 27). This section permits the accused to confess to facts against himself, provided it leads to discovery of information. This is always recorded after warning him that it would be used against him and that too in presence of two important witnesses. This was done. His confession led us to the Janta Commercial College.

To reiterate what the Honourable Judge of the Delhi High Court said, the horrible death of Krishan Sikand remained "unpunished".

Death in the Ait

This account is about the deadly handiwork of terrorists in Canada that remains amongst the worst acts of terror in aviation history. It has been argued though that what happened on 9/11 in New York is the worst. Be that as it may, the Kanishka exploding at 31,000 ft, over the Atlantic Ocean, 130 km off the Irish coast, killing all 307 passengers plus 22 members aboard, was a massive, massive tragedy.

Worse, though the passengers were mainly Canadians, 227 of them were of Indian origin. The investigation was, however, slow to pick up. The Royal Canadian Mounted Police (RCMP) had not invited the CBI to join the investigation for close to a year. It had been plodding along until it was suddenly discovered that the bomb placed in the luggage hold of Flight No. Air India 182 was in the suitcase of a wait-listed passenger with an Indian connection, who was not on the flight.

The hand of the Babbar Khalsa had surfaced. It was then that they also fell back on all information regarding certain Canadians belonging to the Indian diaspora that they had assumed to be desultory intelligence. They had, before 23rd June, 1985 discarded these as unreliable. When Ashok Suri, Superintendent of Police, also of Punjab Cell and I joined the dozen odd RCMP officers working on the Kanishka crash in Toronto, it was almost, to the day, a year after the tragedy struck.

I was in New York in July 1986 on official assignments that had actually just been completed. What took me to New York? It was a year after I took charge as Deputy Inspector General (DIG) and head of the Punjab Cell and I had completed the investigation into the Golden Temple, an Army operation, where a huge cache of illegal weapons had been captured. Additionally, the Army had apprehended nearly 1,500 individuals, including two women, all suspected terrorists.

Investigating the fallout of the operation was huge and, notwithstanding the support team, it had taken a toll on me. I also happened to be the convenor of the working group of DIG level officers of northern states created by the Home Secretary, R. D. Pradhan. This included Deputy Director ranked officers serving with the Intelligence Bureau and RAW of the region. The group worked on information on terrorist activity to counter their plans with thrice-a-week meetings in Chandigarh, which involved travel and commitment.

So, in June 1986, when I was nominated as the country's delegate to participate in the Fourth Symposium of International Terrorism and Unlawful Interferences with Means of Interference at the Paris Headquarters of Interpol, it was a most welcome break of seven days. Subsequently, the Director, CBI allotted more work in continuation of the Paris conference, which would require me to interact with the Scotland Yard in London, FBI and New York Police in New York and the RCMP in Toronto and Ottawa.

It was also June and July, when the schools would be on vacation in India. The children were packed off to my in-laws in Kolkata and my wife and I set off for a trip together to Europe, USA and Canada. We would be back after 25 days or so. I was asked to stay back, however, and my wife returned alone. It so happened that the RCMP Canada sought us out about that time. The Air India disappearance of 23rd June, 1985 was linked to the Babbar Khalsa by the RCMP around then. Its self-proclaimed head, Talwinder Singh Parmar, was supposedly in Patiala. It was thus inevitable that the Punjab Cell, CBI, would become a partner in this investigation.

I was directed to join the RCMP investigations and was told that Ashok Suri, also of Punjab Cell, would assist me. Suri was to join me in New York. Since my wife had to take her flight from the JFK International Airport, I decided to meet Suri at the airport and also finalise arrangements for her to return on her own. To my surprise I saw Suri walking up to me, clearly rattled, escorted by airport security. Though he had landed in the USA, he had no American visa! He only had a Canadian Visa. This was an Air India faux pas for which it was later fined $1,000 by the authorities in the USA.

Police camaraderie found a solution to Suri's visa problem and in a day or two, we both were in Toronto. My wife had to leave on her unhappy, lone, return flight to Delhi as we joined the RCMP team in Toronto. Immediately after Operation Blue Star of June 1984, Canadian terrorists of Indian origin had vowed to avenge the operation. There was no hiding it and Canadian intelligence had received and collated it all. What was the intelligence? There was angry talk in the *gurudwaras* with clear overtones of blowing off Air India planes. Sikh visitors to the *gurudwaras* were warned not to fly Air India.

A Canadian former criminal out of jail told the RCMP that he had been offered $200,000 (Canadian) to place a bomb in an Air India plane and had declined. He named the person who had offered the bag stuffed with cash. It was dismissed as an unreliable exercise. To their credit though, Canadian intelligence bugged the houses of possible suspects and had material to suspect bomb preparations were in progress. One intelligence officer actually saw Inderjit Singh Reyat blowing up an improvised explosive device (IED). The intelligence officer collected the remains of the explosives.

All that information was in vain though. Air India received no alerts. Our High Commission in Ottawa had intelligence officers (RAW) and they were neither alerted nor had they got any inkling on their own. The handling of Air India luggage at Montreal and elsewhere in Canada remained in private hands. The suitcase carrying bombs, booked in the name of a wait-listed transit passenger for Air India 182 took off on flights from Vancouver. The international character of the flight commenced as the Air India aircraft took off from Montreal where the fatal bombs in the name of transit passengers were in the luggage hold, having been offloaded from the Vancouver flight. One was straight away put in the luggage hold of Kanishka and the other also took off from Montreal to be put on an Air India flight from Narita Airport. This one exploded in the hands of the loaders. The death tally went up by two.

The suitcases were booked in two names. The first was a wait-listed transit passenger for Air India 182 from Montreal to London on 23rd June, 1985. The second was on Canadian Pacific Airway in the name of yet another transit passenger flying to Bangkok, taking an Air India flight from Narita Airport, Tokyo on 23rd June, 1985. Both names were fake and, though the passengers never got on the flights, their suitcases were put on flights that they were supposed to take.

Such an act should have never happened and would not have happened even in India in 1985. There was a report that a reluctant loader was persuaded to load this particular suitcase on Air India 182 though the passenger in question was still wait-listed. There was another report that this suitcase was loaded even though it emitted some tell-tale signals of containing explosives. The beeps were ignored by the private handlers. We assiduously applied ourselves to all that was available in the RCMP dossier. Our task was to collect evidence of conspiracy in India.

The Babbar Khalsa existed in India. Before returning to India, I also wanted to meet Prof G. N. Sharma, who was my teacher of English literature both in Maharaja College, Jaipur and Hindu College, Delhi. He was teaching in Canada. An RCMP colleague showed me the passenger list of Air India 182. His younger brother, his sister-in-law and their children had taken the flight from Toronto to Delhi, after spending their holidays with him. Prof Sharma, I was told, had immediately gone to Ireland and then to India. My information was that he was in deep sorrow, almost in a state of depression. He had become a recluse.

There were many Canadians of Indian origin on this flight, whose children were going to visit their grandparents. Their grief would also remain with them all their lives. We returned to India after a quick visit to the Niagara Falls from the Canadian side one weekend. Some hours in the Maid of the Mist, watching the falls, almost within touching distance, wearing our waterproof overalls provided us much mental relief after hours and days poring over material that heightened the sense of horror and sorrow. This visit was organised by a close relative of Ashok Suri. It was a treat that I still remember.

In Delhi, we collected information, data and relevant material on all suspects who had any Indian connection.

Among them were Talwinder Singh Parmar, Inderjit Singh Reyat, Ripudaman Singh Malik, Ajaib Singh Bagri and Hardial Singh Johal. All the material relevant to the bomb placed in the Kanishka luggage hold and those who had knowledge about it and their Indian connections was collated. An officer of the Punjab Cell Deputy Superintendent, R. P. Singh, was all set to give evidence in the trial of all accused involved in bombing Kanishka.

That never happened. The trial of all accused charged with the Kanishka bombing was abruptly dropped. Much of the evidence against them was in their conversations admitting to their roles, obtained through wire taps. In Canadian law it is standard practice for police to bug houses, offices and cars of suspects. That evidence is legal and is routinely used against them in court. However, it is legal evidence in court provided the competent court is approached with material in support before a wiretap is installed and the court's approval obtained prior to the bugging operation.

It so happened in several instances that crucial evidence, thus obtained, was without court orders. The evidence against Inderjit Singh Reyat, Ripudaman Singh Malik, Ajaib Singh Bagri and Hardial Singh Johal was self-incriminatory but in the bugged tapes. The Canadian prosecutors ruled that without legally admissible evidence the charges would be dropped. The entire Kanishka case fell through. The only conviction that took place was of Inderjit Singh Reyat, whose credit card was linked to the bomb that exploded in the hands of two loaders, who were moving it into the Air India plane taking off for Bangkok on 23rd June, 1985 at the Narita Airport, Tokyo. Significantly, he was convicted for lying in court to cover for his co-accused and not for the Kanishka killings. He was never himself tried as an accused. While giving evidence in court as prosecution witnesses, he lied and hence the charge of perjury. He protected the accused tried for the Narita Airport killings. We were not associated with that investigation though. The judge called him an "unmitigated liar".

Reyat was called to depose as his credit card was linked with the purchase of parts that were assembled to make the bomb that exploded, killing two loaders at Narita Airport, Tokyo. Indeed, his conviction was possible only because his credit card was linked to purchases used to assemble the bomb. Talwinder Singh Parmar was killed on 14th October, 1992 in a Punjab Police operation. On 28th January, 2016, an NDTV news report[2] said that Inderjit Singh Reyat had walked out of the prison.

> *"The only person ever convicted over the 1985 Air India bombings … was released from a Canadian prison … after serving two decades behind bars. Inderjit Singh Reyat, a Sikh immigrant, served two-thirds of a nine-year sentence for perjury in one of the deadliest airline attacks in history, said a spokesman for the Parole Board of Canada, confirming his release."*

The death of 329 persons remains unpunished.

---

2   *https://www.ndtv.com/india-news/1985-air-india-kanishka-bombing-indrajit-singh-reyat-released-from-prison-1270837*

Abortive Assassination

The CBI Anti-Terrorist Cell, popularly known as the Punjab Cell, was not even a year old when 31-year old Karamjit Singh, a resident of a village in Patiala District, a diploma holder from an Industrial Training Institute (ITI) Ludhiana, made his lone attempt on the Indian Prime Minister's life. How did Karamjit prepare himself?

Karamjit Singh Singh never made any bones about his desire to kill Rajiv Gandhi and his need for a sophisticated weapon to do this. He was a loner without any seriously thought out plans, a loose-tongued, unbalanced young man, bent on revenge. He loudly proclaimed his intentions but seemed incapable of bringing to fruition his intent to avenge the horrible tragedy that befell his room mate at the hands of an anti-Sikh mob, instigated — to his mind — by Rajiv Gandhi. He was convinced about this.

No one else was convinced about his ability to pull it off and even organised groups, keen on avenging the Blue Star operation and those planning to avenge the Sikh Riots of 1984, cold-shouldered him. His efforts to procure regular arms from those in the business of terror in 1984, 1985 and the better part of 1986 failed. However, his burning desire to avenge his room mate's death did get to a RAW source, who stumbled on this alert on him and worked on it. RAW too did not take him too seriously though. For the source, Karamjit was incidental. He concentrated on his work; the kind RAW required him to do in the area of its domain.

It was 2nd October, 1986. I was in London as a member of the Indian Delegation negotiating an Extradition Agreement with the British government. It is a fact that terrorism that India witnessed from the 1980s triggered a flurry of talks with countries like the U. K. Canada, Germany, UAE and more. There was keenness to agree to extradition agreements with India and I was a member of several delegations. Many a wanted person either lived there or escaped there after committing the crime.

That was when the incident took place. I remember it vividly, as I heard of it over a long distance call from my personal staff. I was ensconced in my room in St James Hotel, London when they reported the story of the near success of the Rajghat attempt on Rajiv Gandhi's life on 2nd October, 1986. A lone gunman had successfully penetrated the sanitised area and had not one, not two but three shots at the Prime Minister. The story was bizarre. "The lone gunman had not been nabbed after his first attempt and had got two opportunities, two hours after his first attempt, to try again." Incredible failure! was my instant reaction.

I rushed back and so did the CBI Director and the Commissioner of Police, Delhi, who were in Vienna as leader and member, respectively, of the Indian team, participating in the annual Interpol Conference. The Delhi Police was the first to reach the scene of crime. The CBI and the Punjab Cell took over the investigation from the Delhi Police within days. What did we find? While Karamjit made no bones about avenging his roommate's death, it was not till July, 1986 that he could procure the weapon, a *'katta'*, from a criminal in Sri Ganganagar, Rajasthan, for ₹300.

The *katta* was a 12-gauge crude sawed off shotgun. He then set about planning his execution. He knew that on 2nd October, his target, Rajiv Gandhi, would be at Rajghat. That is where he planned to make his attempt. Before that he learnt to use the weapon and do some target practice. He actually shot at three human targets in practise, injuring all three in his village. We found that FIRs were registered in all the three cases. Worse, in all the three cases the local police had arrested the 'accused', prosecuted them and also secured their conviction!

When Karamjit procured the *katta*, the RAW source got the information and it was conveyed to Director RAW, who made enquiries. He was briefed well and had learnt a lot about Karamjit. He knew his full name. He knew the name of his village in Patiala district. He knew that he was a diploma holder from a ITI in Ludhiana. He knew the name and address of the factory in Delhi where he was employed till 1984. He also knew that Karamjit planned to hide inside Rajghat! Karamjit's camouflage would be the foliage that the green leaves or the huge bushy growth that the *samadhi* provided then in abundance.

Armed with the information that Karamjit had a '*katta*' and the date and year of his planned attack was 2nd October, 1986, on 27th September, 1986, the Director, RAW informed the Additional Director Intelligence Bureau (IB) in writing: "According to an unverified report, an attempt would be made on the life of our Prime Minister when he goes to Rajghat on October 2nd to lay a wreath on Gandhi's *samadhi*. The would be assassin, a clean-shaved Sikh, was a victim of Delhi riots. He is likely to approach the area in the guise of a *mali* (a gardener) and would hide himself in the bushes nearby."

He did not name Karamjit. He did not mention his factory address or provide his village address. He did not specifically state that he would hide in the trees in Rajghat. All this information would have pinpointed him and facilitated his arrest long before he took his position on a tree inside Rajghat overlooking the area surrounding the Samadhi of Bapu, where VIPs gathered annually to remember the Father of the Nation. The Additional Director IB, reduced this information into a written note and sent it to the Commissioner of Police, Delhi.

The office of the Police Commissioner in turn did a thorough check on the gardeners/*malis* working in Rajghat. None appeared to be a likely assassin. How did Karamjit proceed? Armed with the *katta*, water and dry food, the lone assassin hid on a heavily leafed tree. It looked down on the designated venue where the VIPs would gather on the morning of 2nd October, 1986. He did that for seven days. For his ablutions he used the nights. The full sanitisation of the area that is warranted before the PM visits area accessible to public done just before 2nd October, 1986 failed to detect his presence on the tree. No body climbed the trees or looked into the dense bushes. Nobody!

Karamjit got to make two attempts on Rajiv Gandhi. Once as the PM arrived and once as he left. He missed both times. The first shot was dismissed as a tyre burst by his security, though the PM did remark "it's a gun shot". The second shot, two hours later as the PM returned, also missed him. This time by inches, smashing into the wall as the PM and the President crossed the gates of Rajghat. While the earlier bullet had plunked into a muddy patch harmlessly, the second attempts with two shots fired, hit the brick walls and exposed his presence. The rest is history.

Karamjit was arrested with the Home Minister screaming "shoot him, shoot him" and the DIG Intelligence, Delhi Police, frantically trying to prevent it. He stood up on the tree exposing himself with his hands raised. He had no more bullets. The case went through the due process of the law and he was sentenced as per the court order. Today, having served his sentence, he has made a life for himself, at Patiala, where he is married and has a job. What his act did was to lead to a soul searching within the intelligence agencies.

Karamjit Singh' s attempt to assassinate Rajiv Gandhi was investigated by the Punjab Cell, CBI. It is in the annals of political assassinations, one more case of intelligence failure. Why? The incident raised many questions.

- Was the Delhi Police less than thorough in sanitising Rajghat hours before the Prime Minister visited it?

- How could the assassin, lurking in the tree, overlooking the space where the VIPs would sit for a couple of hours, have been missed?

- Why did the Director RAW not furnish the entire information that was in his possession on Karamjit to the Intelligence Bureau?

- Even if he had done so, would Karamjit have been prevented from even reaching Rajghat?

Why did RAW Chief protect the identity of his source? He chose not to fully disclose all that he knew about Karamjit as he surmised that it would disclose the identity of his source. Once a source is known the source's life is at stake. Also, his utility as informant ends. As a professional, did he act correctly though? It nearly led to another Indian Prime Minister being assassinated while in office.

A Committee under T. N. Seshan, days away from his being appointed Election Commissioner, went into these questions. I, too, appeared before it. The Seshan Committee recommended the creation of Special Protection Group (SPG). This elite force protects our Prime Minister today.

Wanted by the FBI

General A. S. Vaidya retired sometime after the Indian Army completed what is famously remembered as the 'Operation Blue Star', which had lasted from 3rd June to 6th June, 1984. He had settled down with his wife, Bhanumathi Vaidya, in Pune in the comfortable environs of his villa, close to the Rajneesh Ashram. It is in Pune that he met his end at the hands of terrorists.

His killers held a grudge against him for the June 1984 Army Action on the Golden Temple in Amritsar. As early as May 1986, the Bombay Police had alerted him that a terrorist hideout in Antop Hill, Bombay, had yielded intelligence that his Maruti car, registered in the name of Bhanumathi Vaidya, which he used to drive, was being tracked by terrorists. The General started carrying a revolver. He was also given a gun man, Ram Chander Shirsagar.

It all turned out to be of no avail for on 10th August, 1986, as he was carefully driving home from his weekly shopping, two assailants on motor cycles drove up to the driver (the General himself) and shot him in the head, his wife by his side. The Punjab Cell of the CBI was asked to investigate this assassination and we took over the investigation from the Commissioner of Police, Pune. Both the Pune Commissioner of Police and I, as head of Punjab Cell, interacted closely in the investigations.

How the investigation succeeded in zeroing on the killers is another story. Here is an interesting account of how I became a "person of interest" in the eyes of the FBI. Apart from the actual killers, there were several others who were a part of the plan to assassinate the General. The same group had participated in other terrorist crimes in Pune, Mumbai and Udaipur. We learnt two of them had falsified passports, which had American visas and had used them to escape to the United States.

A two-man CBI team comprising an S.P. and a Deputy Superintendent was sent to the USA to join hands with the American Secret Service, who work for Interpol in the USA, as the CBI does in India. The purpose was to locate the terrorists and get them arrested there. Their extradition could follow. They were located, arrested and jailed, pending extradition. No sooner were they arrested that we had word from the American Embassy in Delhi that a federal prosecutor (female) from New Jersey, USA, was arriving. She would conduct the arguments for extradition on behalf of India.

I quickly arranged to collate the material against the two arrested in the USA with the Bombay-Pune Police, the Udaipur Police as well as the CBI. The American prosecutor — they are called District Attorney (DA) there — was unmarried, 40-ish but looked younger. Judy Russell was a demon for work. She had all officers of the CBI, Bombay and Udaipur hopping as she put them through their paces, checking each piece of evidence. Satisfied that we had an iron-clad case for extradition, she went back, leaving us to complete the documentation that would precede extradition.

We got going, preparing what is called the Letter Rogatory. These are documents in support of extradition. They are routed to the foreign competent court through our court. It is a meticulous exercise and one that is the major thrust of any extradition exercise. Once the hearing starts, a support team from India assists the foreign prosecutor, who presents the case in court. Normally, an S.P. of the CBI would have led the support team that would include the investigating officer, a Deputy Superintendent and a CBI prosecutor, apart from him.

In this case, I decided that I ought to do it. There was opposition from the Additional Director, CBI who thought I was trying to wrangle a free foreign trip. The Director, CBI weighed my reasons and approved my proposal. I wanted to be there since the I.B. was sending Ajit Doval, now NSA, then Deputy Director, I.B. The Bureau of Police Research (BPRD) had deputed its Director, the Election Commission, its Deputy Election Commissioner and the Udaipur Police, its Additional Superintendent. Each had a specific role to play during the extradition procedure, should it be required during the hearing.

I believed that the S.P., CBI should be spared the need to offer any "weighty advice", which he, in his relatively junior rank, may find uncomfortable to cope with. Therefore, I went as leader with the S.P. as a part of the team. Since I was the senior CBI officer present and was aware of the evidence, the District Attorney sought me out when she needed any information. We met often during the seven days that the extradition hearing took place. The hearings in New Jersey in January 1988 were held under extreme security.

It was bitterly cold, with sub-zero temperatures. We travelled under armed escort. The persons to be extradited were brought to court handcuffed and their legs shackled. They were kept shackled even in court. They protested but were denied relief by the court hearing the extradition. They appealed. The appeal was heard immediately by a court equivalent to our District Court. The superior court was much better appointed, in furnishing and looks, compared to the extradition court, which was like our magistrate's court! The District Court Judge heard their counsel, inspected the handcuffs and shackles and ordered that they be slightly eased only. The hearing continued and security was tightened. The roofs of our hotel and the court were always swarming with armed men.

I wondered and then assumed that the tight security was deemed necessary because of the large numbers of Khalistan supporters in the USA and Canada. Judy G.

Russell, argued well, repeatedly emphasising the heinous crimes that the men had committed and terror that they were spreading in India and now in the USA. Her interventions were brilliant. A matter of the security of the chain of custody of the fingerprints of one of the proposed extraditees lifted from the scene of crime in Udaipur was questioned too.

The evidence here was weak and she and I had prepared the Additional Superintendent from Udaipur — named Patni — to give evidence in court. His evidence was replete with pauses, because he was trying to gather his thoughts for clarity. The court commented on his pauses but accepted his statement as enough to spike the doubts on the chain of custody. Our entire team watched the hearings, sitting where the jurors sit in court. This was a special privilege that she ensured. The trial court held that both should be extradited and they were after their appeals were exhausted many years later.

Before that and sometime after we returned to India, we learnt to our surprise that the District Attorney who had conducted the extradition had been arrested by the Federal Bureau of Investigation. That was when I learnt that because of threats posted to her, the extradition hearing was held under such tight security cover. The threat letters were investigated by the FBI. She, apparently, thought such a perception would help her to win her case. Then came the bombshell. I received a call from the USA. It was in summer, in June, a Minister ranked officer from our Embassy in the USA, rang me at home. He spoke of the arrest.

The FBI, which was investigating the threats that the DA had received in January during the extradition hearing (of which we had no inkling when we were in New Jersey) had arrested Judy Russell herself for creating a false threat perception. They had found old newspapers from her home with words removed by scissors. These words were pasted together to constitute the various threat letters she had handed over to the FBI. These triggered the security cover during the hearing and the investigation by the FBI. The Minister had been informed by the State Department that the new District Attorney wanted to have a word with the head of the CBI team; that was me.

Of course, that was the formal request. The new District Attorney needed to be briefed. He also said the FBI would talk to me. I wondered if the FBI could be suspecting that I may have had a role in creating the threat perception. Meanwhile, the Ministry of External Affairs alerted the Director, CBI separately. The next thing I saw was the Cabinet Secretary summoning me and the Director, CBI for a meeting in his conference room where, apart from both of us, representatives of IB, RAW, MHA, MEA and PMO were present. The whole case, including the FBI investigation, was discussed threadbare.

The upshot was the decision that I should go to Washington. The man from PMO, Vasudevan, even remarked, 'we will defend you in court!' It was a joke for him and something for others to snigger about but gave me the jitters. So I went to Washington. It was hot and what we, in India, call a "loo", a strong, gusting, feverishly hot, dry summer wind was sweeping the city. I met the new District Attorney and his team and they obtained a full briefing. The FBI officers were present during the briefing but had no uncomfortable questions for me. I will hazard a guess that by the time I arrived they were sure that the previous D.A. had played a lone game.

For me it was a case of much ado about nothing though it gave me a few uneasy nights both in Delhi and Washington. For the US legal system, it created quite a stir because the D.A. was declared to be "insane". In a detailed follow up report, the Washington Post[3] wrote:

> *"A former federal prosecutor (Judy Russell) who faked death threats to herself during proceedings against two suspected Sikh terrorists last year was found not guilty of obstruction of justice by reason of insanity today in U.S. District Court here. Judge Nicholas Politan delivered the verdict against Judy G. Russell, 38, after Justice Department lawyers presented psychiatric reports stating that she is severely disturbed and a possible schizophrenic with as many as four distinct personalities."*

---

3   *https://www.washingtonpost.com/archive/politics/1989/03/11/ex-prosecutor-found-insane-in-case-of-faked-threats/b2ebc90f-0205-4949-847a-46019cc8ff1e/*

The story ran thus: in February 1988, Judy Russell, informed the federal magistrate overseeing the extradition hearings that she had received three death threats related to the case. FBI agents, however, began to suspect that Russell had fabricated the threats when she said a fourth note warning "Federal Court Death for you" was slipped under her hotel door. U.S. marshals reported that nobody had approached her room.

Agents matched the typewritten letters on her 1983 federal job application to lettering on envelopes in which the threats had been mailed. Agents searched her home and found unmailed threats and glue, scissors and plastic gloves with ink smudges that matched the ink on the threats. Russell insisted that she did not remember mailing the threats or know how the other notes appeared in her home. This, according to government psychiatrists, was consistent with her mental state.

Friends and colleagues describe Russell as an ingenious and driven attorney who, throughout her life, had shown a knack for impressing the right people at the right time. The U.S. District Court Judge, Nicholas Politan, ordered Russell to report for psychiatric evaluation at an outpatient clinic. The verdict marked the downfall of a woman once mentioned by New Jersey politicians as a candidate for public office.

For me, it was time to heave a sigh of relief that I did not get embroiled in any needless controversy.

An Act of Circumvention

When you have worked in the Central Bureau of Investigation, also called the Bureau, for as long as I have (33+) years, you do remember incidents that have more than a passing interest. This is one such story, with all the elements of high drama. It has a foreign hand, it involves the highest in the land, no less than the Prime Minister himself intervening. It also involves a terrorist crime interfacing with Indian diplomacy, with the crime coming off second best. All this happened in the 1980s.

On 31st October, 1984, Indira Gandhi was assassinated by her bodyguards. A bloodbath was unleashed in the aftermath of the killing, the repercussions of which were felt for many unfortunate years. It was some three years or so after the assassination that this incident took place in Srinagar. This was when terrorism was almost at its fag end. A British citizen of Indian origin, a former Member of the House of Commons, an academic, a confidante of Margaret Thatcher, then British Prime Minister and a member of the Conservative Party was in jail in Srinagar because we found his activities were encouraging terrorist crime in our border state.

There was enough evidence to prosecute him under our anti-terrorist laws. It was then that the CBI, Director, Mohan G. Katre, directed me to meet the Minister of Internal Security. He added, for good measure, that I ask the legal adviser of the Punjab Cell to accompany me. I was the Deputy Inspector General, who was heading the CBI's Anti Terrorist Cell, better known as the Punjab Cell. I was also reporting to the Director, CBI. It was early winter and we were directed by the Special Assistant (S. A.) to the Minister to reach his office in North Block by 11 am.

The Minister was a bureaucrat when it came to files. He needed no briefing. The Home Secretary was already in the room. The issue was how to drop the charges against the don, then in judicial custody in Srinagar and send him back to the U.K. Margaret Thatcher, had spoken to the Indian Prime Minister, Rajiv Gandhi, and the decision was to free this British subject of Indian origin as quickly as possible. This, in brief, was our information. I thought that with the law empowering the government to withdraw criminal cases against any one sought to be prosecuted, there was hardly anything that the CBI could do in this case.

Then came the twister. The government did not want to exercise its power of withdrawal. It wanted the CBI to drop the charges. The Minister was a criminal lawyer. He knew the law. While criminal investigations can be started by any investigation agency, it has no legal authority to close any investigation without the trial court endorsing its prayer. Further, the prayer for Closure of Investigation can only be made if the investigation finds that no crime has been committed. Here was a case where the evidence to file a chargesheet was foolproof. The CBI could not seek Closure of Investigation on the ground there was no material to prosecute.

The trial court would, in the normal course, read our case diaries and find so much evidence that not only would it turn down our prayer but would certainly pass strictures on the prayer as being blatantly dishonest. Further conversation also made it clear that since the last word is always that of the court, even if the government withdrew the case, the court could turn it down in the face of the unassailable material to launch prosecution. If the court did that, it would be a huge embarrassment all round. We were literally on the horns of a dilemma. A diplomatic potpourri was brewing.

Clearly, the Minister was not seeking any answer. He wanted a failsafe operation. We withdrew, assuring him that we would come back in a couple of hours with some answers. The lawns of the North Block were inviting, though it was early winter. We paced the lawns and applied ourselves to the issue at hand. Two hours later, with no sure solution but with a bit of brass and bluster in our minds, we returned. If we had to pull it off, active involvement of others was necessary, I suggested. What did I have in mind? The Minister asked me to spell it out.

I told him that the CBI must be advised in a communication that the government desired that proceedings against the former British M. P. be dropped. In other words, the Home Secretary has to advise the Director, CBI that, for diplomatic reasons, the government of India has to send back the accused to the U. K. I said that we could then file a report in the trial court in Srinagar narrating the evidence collected and annex the Home Secretary's advice and request the honourable court to drop proceedings. I further suggested that the Chief Secretary, J&K (CS) be kept in the loop. The audience demurred but I persisted. A little discussion later, the Home Secretary's buy-in was secured. The Minister then said that while the J&K C. S. would be in the loop, I would personally have to interact with him to ensure that there were no slip-ups.

I was asked to fly to Srinagar as soon as possible and meet the Chief Secretary, whom I knew. Two days later, a special flight took me to Srinagar. The Chief Secretary heard me patiently. He then sat back and drummed his table for a long time. I waited. It was a longish wait before he made up his mind. Then he acted with alacrity. He sent for the Divisional Commissioner, Srinagar. While we waited, he said that she would deal with this situation. She would pull it off too, he said with great confidence. This lady was a firebrand and a friend of the District Judge, Srinagar. She was best placed to act in this unusual matter. He proved correct. I am glossing over the rest for obvious reasons.

A recently retired Foreign Secretary of our government, later to be Lt Governor Delhi and also Governor, Uttar Pradesh, kept himself apprised. He was the emissary of Mrs Thatcher. He interacted with me and kept himself posted about the matter. He arranged to pick up our accused from Srinagar as soon as he was released. He put him on a direct flight from Delhi to Heathrow and that was the end of the matter.

Breaching the
Chinese Walls

I was Deputy Inspector General Coordination in the CBI in 1989. The CBI's Interpol division, the CBI Academy, the Antiques Unit and the Narcotics Cell reported to me through their superintendents. This was a far less hectic charge to which I had moved in early 1989. My previous charge of the Punjab Cell involved a scorching pace of action, working and travelling seven days a week, moving not only between my headquarters in Delhi and Chandigarh, my battle ground against terrorists, but to wherever terrorists struck and the Punjab Cell was directed to investigate.

After four years of this feverish pace, my wife pointed out that I was giving no time to the children, my two teenage daughters and a younger son. I mentioned this to the Director, CBI, who gave me this lighter charge within a fortnight. He posted the DIG Co-ordination as DIG Punjab Cell and posted me in his place. Around this time, China was in the throes of democratic stirrings. The youth in China, led by writings and words of student leaders, were upping the ante in several pro-democracy strikes. This demand started in 1980 and, though most of the student leaders were jailed, the movement continued. March 1989 began to see a large gathering of pro-democracy students at the Tiananmen Square.

The protests were precipitated by the death of pro-reform Communist general secretary, Hu Yaobang, in April 1989. Eventually, the government declared martial law and sent in the People's Liberation Army on 4th June, 1989. It moved in with assault rifles and tanks against the students demanding pro-democratic reforms. Several thousand demonstrators were killed by the army on 4th and 5th June, 1989. The international community, human rights organisations and political analysts condemned the Chinese government for the massacre. For the purposes of our story, what is relevant is that the crackdown stripped Beijing of the honour of hosting the October 1989 International Interpol Conference.

These annual conferences are planned years in advance. Beijing had been preparing for at least three years to organise the annual Interpol conference. This peremptory pull back by the world was a loss of face. Not to be outdone, China responded by promptly announcing the Asian Regional Drug Law Enforcement Symposium in 1989 itself. Invitations, both formal and personal, were sent to Asian and Middle East countries. No western country was invited as none would have accepted, I am sure.

India was uncertain about whether or not to accept. However, there was a line of thinking that it would be unwise to ignore the Chinese that ultimately prevailed. The government of India, however, stipulated that the Indian delegation would be a low key one and comprise no more than three delegates. It was also the government's fiat that a CBI officer would lead the delegation and the other two would be from the Delhi Police and Indian Customs.

As DIG in charge of the narcotics cell, I was nominated as leader, a good 20 days or so before the conference was to begin. It was the grapevine that carried the news to me. There were barely seven days for the conference to start and I checked with someone who kept track of the Director's orders. He was non-committal. Meanwhile, my colleagues for the conference from the Delhi Police and Customs were making enquiries because they had received their go-ahead orders 20 days ago. They had all the papers and were on the way to get their visas and tickets.

It was then that I learnt that a senior person in the CBI was unhappy that he had not been nominated by the Director. Since he was just a rank junior to the Director, he felt that if the Director could not head the delegation, he should. A China visit would be an unlikely opportunity in the normal course. He was, therefore, trying to persuade the Director to change the nomination in his favour. His argument was that even with him leading, it would be a low key presence. He did not transmit the file to me, hoping that he would make it to the conference. Apparently, the government did not agree.

Finally, the file trickled down to me and had to be processed in just three days before the conference was to begin. Luckily, the Financial Advisor, Home, and I had shared a Sikkim tenure and were on excellent terms. What normally would have taken a few days to move from table to table in the Ministry of Home Affairs was cleared in 30 minutes. Visa and tickets followed because the authorities had been spoken to in advance.

I made it to the conference just in time though I did not travel with the delegation. It had reached a day in advance like most other delegates. My flight from Delhi to Bangkok was by Air India and from there to Beijing was by the Chinese National Airways. It was the most austere of aircrafts, unlike any I had ever travelled by. It did not even have a carpet; only the bare necessities. For lunch it served just noodles. The Beijing airport was even less eye-catching. The city seemed to have few pedestrians, fewer cars and hundreds of cyclists. Beijing was far removed from what it is today. For purposes of the conference, of course, arrangements were five-star, beginning with the hotel, which had spacious rooms. Breakfast was included in the tariff that the government bore.

The other arrangements and scheduling were at par with any other annual Interpol Conference but everything by way of hospitality was jazzed up for effect. The minister of China's Ministry of the Interior inaugurated the conference. He was old and required two people to walk on either side. His voice, however, belied his old mien; it was imposing. When he hosted a banquet for the delegates with a 47-course dinner — fish and ducks severally cooked — he walked unaided to each table to clink glasses.

During the conference, the Iranian delegates were accorded a special welcome. When they spoke, the host country was all ears. This marked attention was interesting and probably driven by Iran's animosity for the west. From India, the three of us were active participants. The other two with me were Amod K. Kanth, DCP Delhi and S. K. Goel, Assistant Collector Customs. Both went on to distinguish themselves, the former as DGP and subsequently the General Secretary of the NGO, Prayas. The latter became Chairman, Board of Customs. Goel was elected as Secretary of the conference. It was he who drafted my speech as head of the mission, which received accolades.

Clearly, the Chinese were all out to impress the guests. They were gracious hosts, effusive in their show of friendship. There were many official lunches and dinners, not to mention the excursions to the Great Wall, the Forbidden City and other spots of tourist interest. There was also a visit to the Police Show with a parade and exercises and a musical experience at a public theatre. The *bandobast* was *pucca*. Our air-conditioned buses were given unimpeded passage. A three-hour journey to the Great Wall was completed in slightly less than half the time.

Even while giving full attention to details around the conference, the underlying attempt seemed to be to convey the story that all was fine with China. That was the clear priority. My experiences with two previous international conferences, at Tokyo in 1979 and Paris in 1986, were quite different. Tokyo did have some travel but no freebies. Paris was austere. No tourist jaunts anywhere. For Beijing the aim was to paint over the 'other' face that had won it such notoriety. That was easier said than done and I personally had an opportunity to experience the 'other' face.

One morning I found myself with an excruciating back pain. It was sudden, unexpected and I had to see a doctor in the general hospital. The hospital was one antiseptic hole; there were lots of paramedics with a team of white-coated doctors in attendance and hardly any patients. I was not a sleuth for nothing and soon managed to espy a crowd of people and patients jostling in long queues in the same hospital, cleverly segregated from the part to which I was taken. I was nosey and China's very keenness to show what was patently untrue revealed volumes to me.

The class distinction became more apparent when it came to the currencies. The reforms of the 1980s had led to a market economy that favoured some more than the others, leading to a two-currency regime with the Yuan and the Renminbi (also called the People's Currency). The distinction was subtle: while the Renminbi remained the official currency of China as the medium of exchange, the

Yuan was the unit of account of the country's economic and financial system. The point was that the Renminbi did not work in the posh stores!

There could be no worse form of segregation than the less privileged Chinese population having to suffer the indignity of not being able to use their own money freely in their own country. This became obvious in our interactions with our interpreters. They were always keen to exchange our Yuans for their Renminbi because only the Yuan gave them access to the state-run Friendship Stores to which the underprivileged locals had no access. Only the Yuan was the legal tender for these stores. The Yuan was given to foreigners and a select few.

The Friendship Stores sold exclusively to foreign visitors and tourists, diplomats and government officials and stocked what was not available locally; mostly foreign goods. It suited us because we wanted to take back indigenous goods only and our interpreters bought them with their Renminbi. We settled by squaring up with our Yuans. They were ecstatic with our Yuans in their hands. These restrictions no longer prevail.

We had an unforgettable trip. The question is did China live down the Tiananmen horror? Will the world not see similar horrors again? The Uyghurs are facing cleansing drives and the pro-democracy movement in Hong Kong are truths unfolding before the world. The Chinese state continues to be at loggerheads with democracy; even though the skies are bluer in Beijing and there is every sign of pomp and glamour.

The Missing Mughal *Mohur*

A little history on Islamic coins is relevant to this story on a big Mughal coin that went missing. It is about the largest such coin in the world. Dr Michael Bates, Curator of Islamic Coins, American Numismatic Society, New York, has studied and written extensively about Islamic coins. Among other well regarded writers are two Indians, P. L. Gupta, who wrote 'Mughal Coins, A Review' and S. H. Hodivata, who wrote 'Gigantic Coins'.

The coins are of enormous value because of the sheer skill that went into their coinage. The two authors write about the practice of Muslim rulers in the South Asian subcontinent giving large presents by way of coins. They also admit there is no evidence of large coins in India until the time of the Mughal Emperor Akbar. The story of the two gold *mohurs*, which the Special Investigation Unit XI of the CBI was asked to locate, features gigantic coins of the era of Emperor Jahangir and Shahjahan.

More than Akbar, it was Jahangir who took a special interest in coins and conceived the idea of issuing coins for regular circulation, each with the Zodiac sign appropriate to the month of its issue. The inscriptions on the coins, in both Arabic and Persian scripts, required numerous hammer blows, which strained the technical resources of the mint. It was a difficult task to fully bring out the inscriptions along the outer edge of each piece of the coin. Repeated hammer blows were necessary to strike the mass of the metal to clearly bring out the Arabic and Persian letters.

No wonder the craftsmen in the mint — Dr Bates calls them 'minters' — were highly paid. In Jahangir's time it was ₹700 a month! These large coins have now mostly disappeared. The two coins that belong to India and survive lie in the vault of a foreign bank. This story is still relevant because, I believe, that the coins must be brought home. In November 1987, one of our Embassies or High Commissions in Europe alerted the government and the CBI that two gold coins of Mughal origin had been put up for auction in Geneva.

The Paris-based Banque Indosuez, through its Geneva Branch, had asked the world famous auctioneer, Habsburg Feldman SA, to auction two gold coins, aka *asharphis* or *mohurs*. One was a large coin, the world's largest, and the other was relatively small. The auction was planned on November 9, 1987 at the Moga Hotel, Geneva. There was scant information about them with the CBI. The CBI, therefore, undertook enquiries. The search for historical details of the coins in question revealed some interesting information on the large coin.

- It was created at the time of Emperor Jahangir.
- It weighed 11,935.8 grams and comprised one thousand gold coins.
- It was 20.3 cms in diameter.
- It was minted in Agra in 1613.
- It was valued at $16 million in 1987.

Historical records prove that Emperor Jahangir had minted only two such gold coins. One was presented by him to the King of Iran, when its Ambassador visited the court of Jahangir. The other one remained with the Mughals. During the reign of Aurangzeb, this coin became the property of his Nizam, who was the Administrator and the Mughal Emperor's viceroy for Hyderabad.

Hyderabad then comprised today's Andhra and Telangana and parts of Karnataka. When Emperor Aurangzeb, who ruled for 49 years (born 3rd November 1618; died March 1707) sent his third son, Prince Mohammed Azam, to capture Bijapur, the army had been on the verge of being starved out at one stage. At that critical time, Ghazi ud-din Khan Feroze Jung I, saved it by sending grain. He was helpful in many other ways during this prolonged battle. Out of gratitude, Aurangzeb presented the large coin to him after emerging victorious.

Long after Aurangzeb's death in 1707, the Mughal Empire broke up. In July 1774, Ghazi ud-Din's son Mir Qamar-Uddin declared himself the independent ruler of Hyderabad and his dynasty, the Jah dynasty, took over. That was the dynasty ruling Hyderabad at the time of

India's Independence. He called himself Nizam-I and his descendants continued to call themselves Nizams. The Jah dynasty continued till 7th September, 1948. The last Nizam, Oman Ali Khan, was Nizam-VII.

The large coin in question (made from one thousand gold coins) remained with the Jah dynasty till the very end. The smaller coin was minted in Lahore by Emperor Shahjahan in 1639. It comprised 100 gold coins. It weighed a little more than 900 grams and it was 9.3 cms in diameter. History tells us of many such coins. For the Nizam, whose riches were legendary, to have had one is not unusual.

The CBI Special Investigation Unit XI investigated cases dealing with antique theft. It was headed by a Superintendent rank officer in 1987 and the unit reported to the Deputy Inspector General (DIG). I assumed charge as DIG of this unit in 1989. This unit had registered an FIR (first information report) under the provisions of the Antique and Art Treasures Act 1972, theft under section 380 of the Indian Penal Code and under section 120(B) also of the Indian Penal Code (Conspiracy) on 13th November, 1987.

I reviewed the case and found from documents collected by the lawyers of the Banque Indosuez — the unit that conducted the investigation, when they had come to Hyderabad in 1989 for their case of attachment of the assets of Mukarram Jah — that the auction effort in November in 1987 had preceded the granting of a loan of Swiss Franc (CHF) 9 million in 1988 to Mukarram Jah. It was clear that the loan was negotiated when the auction failed. From correspondence between the bank and Mukarram Jah, it was also evident that the two gold coins were pledged to the bank.

The data collected in the course of the investigations at Hyderabad threw up enough information to confirm that gold coins were pledged to the Banque Indosuez, Geneva, by Mukarram Jah. The CBI also found that Mukarram Jah registered two companies in the British Virgin Islands, British Overseas Territory in the Caribbean. They were named Crystalor Services and Tamarind Corporation. These were set up to carry out sheep farming in Western Australia. The loan of CHF 9 million was shown to have been made to these two companies, some CHF 7 million to Crystalor and about CHF 2 million to Tamarind.

These details and much more were available in documents and papers — both filed in the Hyderabad City Civil Court by the lawyers of Banque Indosuez, Geneva — and from the documents in their possession. It was also clear that, as early as 1987 November, Mukarram Jah had tried to auction these two gold coins. He expected to raise about CHF 9 million from this auction. For many reasons, possibly including the CBI setting the law into motion in November 1987, no further attempts to auction them were made.

During the investigations I learnt from my sources that one partner of the auctioning firm, Dr Geza Von

Hapsburg, had visited Delhi in February 1988, for the first time, a few months after the auction in November 1987 had failed to throw up a purchaser for the coins. He also met one Dr Partha Bannerjea in Calcutta, who was known to be a person interested in coins and art objects. They knew each other from the sixties when Dr Bannerjea was a student in Heidelberg, where Von Hapsburg was also a student.

Von Hapsburg visited Delhi and Calcutta where Dr Bannerjea, a well-known homoeopathy doctor, was requested to find buyers for the two gold coins. He came twice, once in February-March 1988 and again in May-July 1988, Dr Bannerjea told us. Von Hapsburg told Dr Bannerjea that these gold coins belonged to the former Nizam. It is unfortunate that the CBI did not know about his visits. He would surely have been arrested as a receiver of stolen property as per the FIR filed by the CBI. He was in India to sell the gold coins! What an opportunity missed.

I must confess that in 1989, when I learnt of Dr Geza Von Hapsburg's efforts to find buyers in India, I could have initiated steps to entrap him into making another attempt so that he could be apprehended and questioned. That too did not happen as it did not strike me at that time. Investigations in Western Australia, a sheep-farming area of Australia, confirmed that Mukarram Jah's efforts at sheep farming had come to a naught. Hence the bank had started the legal proceedings against him in Hyderabad.

With this material being available my proposed trip to West Australia along with the Chief Investigating Officer to collect evidence was no longer required. The investigations and enquiries were thereafter carried out in Geneva. The Additional Director, CBI, A. P. Mukherjee, proceeded to Geneva and, with the help of our Embassy officers in Geneva, he established contact with the Federal Department of Justice and Police, Switzerland. His contact there was Dr Lionel Frei, Section Chief, International Legal Cooperation. The CBI's contention that the two gold coins were the property of the government of India was forcefully put across by the Additional Director, CBI. He informed Dr Frei that when Hyderabad merged with India in September 1948, the then Nizam, who was the seventh ruler, made a list of his personal properties that would be retained by him. It included his palaces, his lands and his personal wealth, which were astronomical. He later converted a better part of his wealth into 24 trusts. What was listed out was his personal wealth. The two gold coins were not included as a part of his personal wealth.

All that was not part of the list became state property and belonged to the government of India. The CBI position was that since the two gold coins belonged to the government of India, Switzerland should treat this case as one dealing with stolen property. Dr Frei did not accept this proposition though. The gold coins were not in the actual physical possession of the government of India, he pointed out and, under Swiss Criminal law, the CBI did not have any case of theft. At no stage were the two gold coins ever in possession of the government of India. How could they then be stolen?

He advised the filing of a Civil suit in Geneva to claim the gold coins. There was an effort by the CBI to persuade the Department of Culture, Government of India, to make this an issue between Switzerland and India. That did not make any headway. The coins have still not been recovered.

The Elephant
in the Courtroom

The one elephant that I choose to write about is connected with the 1993 serial bomb blast in Bombay, now Mumbai. The were 12 blasts that took place on Friday, 12th March, 1993. In a space of barely two hours, they ripped Bombay apart, killing nearly 300 and injuring some 1,400+ seriously. There were, however, 13 bombs mentioned by the Bombay Police. The 13th did not go off. The real story is that the 13th blast was a plant and was shown to have gone off in a Muslim-dominated area. All done for a good cause; to avert any communal violence!

It was decided by the government of India that the CBI would investigate the blasts. A Special Task Force (STF) was set up within the CBI and I was given additional charge, as its Joint Director. I was then Joint Director (Anti-Corruption). The state government thought that it would conduct a probe too, as it would allow it to be better informed of such crimes, the taking over of the investigation was postponed till the state filed what, in police parlance, is known as an 'incomplete chargesheet'.

The Bombay police chargesheeted 189 persons under the Terrorist and Disruptive Activities (Prevention) Act (TADA) and various other offences under the Indian Penal Code such as murder, conspiracy, waging war against the state and such others. After the CBI took charge, it continued the investigation, as permissible under the Criminal Procedure Code and collected more evidence. In the process, the CBI arrested nine members of the Dawood gang and found evidence to link Pakistan and ISI with the crime.

The CBI's continued investigation also amassed material in support of the charges already made out by the Bombay Police. We filed 17 more supplementary chargesheets, adducing more by way of evidence, exhibits and opinion. Besides, we arrested 15 to 16 absconders. There were more than 20 of them; many of them had fled the country to Pakistan, the UAE and Portugal. We then presented it all before the trial court through upwards of 800 witnesses, experts and investigating officers and thousands of exhibits.

We also dropped a major charge under section 121, Indian Penal Code that alleged that the accused had waged war against the state, as we found no evidence to sustain this charge. Eventually, in 2012, a large majority of them were tried and more than a hundred were sentenced to various terms of imprisonment, including life. Some were sentenced to death, though finally only one, Yakub Memon, was hanged. The absconders continue to be arrested in India and abroad; Abu Salem from Portugal and recently from the UAE. Pakistan denied their presence.

During our investigation to nail all Dawood's accomplices, one name, Iqbal Mirchi — full name Mohammed Iqbal Memon — became linked to these blasts. He was born in Mumbai on 25th April, 1950. He and members of his family were given the surname '*Mirchi*' as this Memon family did business in spices. Our investigations found material pointing to him as Dawood's man, responsible for Dawood's illicit drug business in Asia, Africa and Europe. Had he helped in procuring the explosives, arms and other logistics for the Mumbai blasts and the riots?

Mirchi had houses in Mumbai and in London, where he was staying at the time. After preliminary investigations, we obtained court orders for searching his houses at both places. The London searches were conducted by Scotland Yard. Both the searches drew blanks to link him with the blasts. However, the searches conducted by Scotland Yard, where Joint Director, P. C. Sharma — who later became Director, CBI — was present, threw up material linking him closely to the then Chief Justice, Bombay High Court.

Without going into specifics, suffice it to say that substantial financial transactions in dollars and pounds between the two were clearly established. There were emails, as prima facie evidence, of attempts to camouflage the payment of illegal gratification as a transaction between an author and his publisher. Imagine the contours of the case! The highest in the judiciary in Bombay had been compromised in the matter of a trial, which would be done in a court subordinate to him. Was corrupting the judiciary also included in Dawood's grand plan to avenge the Babri Masjid demolition?

It appeared that some $25,000 (or pounds), already paid to Chief Justice, Bombay High Court, was proposed to be regularised on instructions of Iqbal Mirchi, to his man in London, one S. S. Musafir. Iqbal Mirchi's mail to him told him that he, as Chief Executive Officer (CEO) of Roebuck Publishing House, had to make available certain documents. This document would reflect that Mr S. S. Musafir — CEO of Roebuck Publishing House — and the Chief Justice, Bombay High Court, had agreed that this publishing house would pay a royalty of $80,000 for the rights of publication and sale abroad of his book, 'Muslim Law and the Constitution', for a period of two years.

The $25,000 (or pounds) was an advance against this agreement. The e-mail specified that the Chief Justice, Bombay High Court, had asked Iqbal Mirchi for these documents. It appeared, subject to detailed investigation, that Roebuck Publishing House was itself created for this subterfuge. The planned role of Iqbal Mirchi then emerged as more sinister than funding explosives. He had been assigned the role of corrupting the judiciary by Dawood. Of this, I was confident. I brought these documents to the knowledge of the Director, CBI. I believe that the Director had briefed the then CJI.

However, fresh developments gave a bizarre twist to our findings. The Bombay and Maharashtra Bar intervened and the whole matter came up before the Supreme Court of India and a two-member Supreme Court Bench heard this matter under the citation C. Ravichandran Iyer vs Justice A. M. Bhattacharya and others. It appears that the Bombay Bar Association (BBA), the Bar Council of Maharashtra and Goa (BCIMG) and the Advocates Association of Western India (AAWI) sought the CJI Bombay's resignation. What were their grounds?

To quote them from the Supreme Court order:

"…though the first respondent (CJI Bombay, Justice A. M. Bhattacharjee) had in his custody documents to show that 1ˢᵗ respondent had negotiated with Mr S. S. Musafir, Chief Executive of Roebuck Publishing, London and the acceptance by the 1ˢᵗ respondent for publication and sale abroad of a book authored by him viz. 'Muslim Law and the Constitution' for two years at a royalty of $80,000 (eighty thousand US dollars) and an inconclusive negotiation for US$75,000 (Seventy five thousand US dollars) for overseas publication of his book 'Hindu Law and the Constitution' (2ⁿᵈ edition) he did not divulge the information but kept confidential. From about late 1994, there was considerable agitation among members respondents of 3 (BBA) and 4 (AAWI)

that certain persons whose names were known to all and who were seen in the court and were openly talked about were bringing influence over the 1ˢᵗ respondent and could 'influence the course of judgement of the former Chief Justice of Bombay'.

It was also rumoured the former Chief Justice Bombay has been paid a large some of money in foreign exchange purportedly as royalty for a book written by him viz 'Muslim Law and the Constitution'. The amount of royalty appeared to be totally disproportionate to what a publisher abroad would be willing to pay for a foreign publication of a book which might be of academic interest within India (since the book was a dissertation of Muslim Law in relation to the Constitution of India). There was a growing suspicion at the Bar that the amount might have been paid for reasons other than the ostensible reason."

As the 1ˢᵗ respondent's (then the incumbent CJI, Bombay) efforts to explain his conduct to them and the Advocate General Maharashtra did not cut much ice, the demand for his resignation continued. It was then that C. Ravichandran Iyer, an advocate, moved a writ under Article 32 of the Constitution of India, seeking to prevent BBA, BCIMG, AAWI from coercing his resignation. The demand was that the Chief Justice, Bombay High Court, Mr A. M. Bhattacharjee, not be allowed to resign but for the CBI to investigate him instead, followed by impeachment proceedings.

The Supreme Court Bench in its order dated 05/09/1995, written by Justice K. Ramaswamy, relying on a host of interpretations of statute, regulation and observations of Judges of the American Supreme Court, ruled that it would be the peers of the tainted judge who would take action on his alleged misconduct. To quote,

> *"Bearing all the above in mind, we are of the considered view where the complaint relates to the judge of a high court, the Chief Justice of the High Court, after verification and, if necessary, after confidential enquiry from his independent source, should satisfy himself about the truth of the imputations made by the Bar Association through its office bearers against the judge and consult the Chief Justice of India, where deemed necessary, by placing all the information before him and when the Chief Justice of India is seized of the matter, to avoid embarrassment to him and to allow fairness in the procedure to be adopted in furtherance thereof, the Bar should suspend all further action to enable the Chief Justice of India to appropriately deal with the matter".*

It went on to say:

> *"This procedure would not only facilitate nipping in the bud the conduct of a judge leading to loss of public confidence in the courts and sustain public faith in the efficacy of the rule of law and respect for the judiciary and would also avoid needless embarrassment of contempt proceedings against office bearers of the Bar*

*Association and group libel against all concerned. They,
his peers, will decide the course of action against him."*

In other words there never shall be any investigation by the CBI or any other agency against any judge of any High Court or the Supreme Court ever. In the present case the final sentence reads:

"Since the first respondent (CJI Bombay High Court) has already demitted the office, as we have stated as above, so that it could form a precedent for the future. The writ petition is disposed off accordingly."

The elephant here is corruption in the higher echelons of the judiciary. The Supreme Court of India, in its infinite wisdom, has laid a procedure to tackle this corruption, which permanently bars outside investigation of any High Court/Supreme Court judge. This elephant is going nowhere. It remains in the room of the CJI, India.

Since then, at least four judges, one from Delhi High Court, one from Karnataka, one from the Lucknow Bench of the Allahabad Court and one from Punjab and Haryana High Court have come under adverse notice. A recently retired judge from Odisha is under investigation by the CBI. Justice Ramaswamy's judgement makes the CJI the final authority where a judge's conduct is in question. Surely, a rap on the wrists is not going to stop big corruption in the higher judiciary. Is it time to revisit Justice Ramaswamy's judgement?

A little insight into the background of the former Chief Justice of the Bombay High Court, is called for. He was born in July 1933 and became a very successful advocate of the Siliguri District Court. Ananda Mohan Bhattacharjee went on to become the Legal Advisor to the Chogyal of Sikkim. Without practising in any High Court, he became a High Court judge from the bar. His help was invaluable to the government of India when bitter negotiations were going on between the Chogyal of Sikkim and the government of India.

Sikkim joined the Indian union on 16th May, 1975. When the Sikkim High Court was established, he became its first puisne judge. Later, he became its Acting Chief Justice. He was made Chief Justice of the Bombay High Court from 1993 to 1995. In 1994, the Bar made the charges. When confronted by the Bar and others, he explained that he had failed to check the bona fides of the publisher. He apologised. He assured the AG Maharashtra that he would go on leave, recuse himself from the hearings for the remaining few months of his tenure but the Bar was inflexible. He resigned.

Incidentally, both the judge and the drug baron are no more. Iqbal Mirchi remained in London, where he died in 2013 and the judge passed away in Kolkata in 2008.

Capricious Courts and Free Felons

On 6th November, 1997, the Supreme Court Bench of Justices M. Mukherjee and K.Thomas refused to impose criminal charges, jail sentences and fines against the BJP Member of Parliament, Brij Bhushan Saran Singh and dropped criminal charges and fines imposed on Union Minister, Kalpanath Rai, Minister of State for Power (Independent Charge) and Saboo V. Chacko, Regional Manager, East West Airlines, the East West Airlines (referred to as the company).

Their interpretation of the law of the land and how it is applied to law breakers seemed suspiciously different from the basis on which the CBI had investigated a critical case or how the Special Judge, trying the case, had. The CBI and the Special Judge of the Terrorist and Disruptive (Prevention) Act (TADA), had interpreted it in unison; to spell imprisonment or fine for the Minister and the corporate/company.

This decision came after months of investigation, followed by months of trial, an exhaustive investigation and detailed study of evidence, respectively. This Bench of the Supreme Court in its wisdom found the case was weak against the more powerful and influential amongst the accused and let them off the hook, finding a strange way to convict the weakest among the charged. In the process it contradicted its own position in the same case!

Worse, in one stroke, it calmly nullified the entire CBI investigation, which meant the hard work of collecting criminal information, collecting exhibits and documents, tracing witnesses and recording their statements U/S 161 Code of Criminal Procedure (CrPC). All this was reduced to a big zero and rendered totally irrelevant.

In effect, the Special Judge, TADA Court — who considered all this evidence as relevant and sent to jail or fined the 10 arraigned, including a minister — too was declared an illiterate in law for having accepted the CBI investigation and pronouncing judgement, convicting 10 of the 12 accused arraigned before the judge by the CBI.

The TADA, an anti-terrorist law, had been in force from 1985 to 1995 in the whole of India. For purposes of abundant clarification here, on 25th May, 1993, Section 3 of this act was expanded by adding sub section 5, whereby being a member of a gang and committing terrorist acts became punishable as well.

After the serial Bombay blasts of 1993, when the full force of law set about arresting Dawood Ibrahim, the rest of the gang leaders, Mohammed Dosa, Tiger Memon and their followers ran helter-skelter. Every state police was on the lookout for them. So was the Delhi Police.

On 23rd July, 1993 at 4 am, a Crime Branch team of the Delhi Police laid hands on five members of Dawood Ibrahim's gang, travelling in two Toyota cars, on an alert. They had arms on them. These weapons were lethal. They included pistols, hand grenades and button knives. Obviously, they were planning a terrorist act.

Those apprehended were:

1. Subhas Singh Thakur
2. Gyanender Thakur
3. Syam Kishore Garikapaty
4. Chandrakant Patil
5. Paras Mohan Desai.

On 27th July, 1993, the investigation was handed over to the CBI. As Joint Director, CBI Special Task Force, a unit created within the CBI to investigate terrorist crimes, I took charge of the investigation. My job was to establish that they were a gang; that they were involved in terrorist crimes; to locate other members of the gang and, very importantly, to apprehend those who gave them protection, food, shelter and other logistical support in Delhi.

This work proceeded apace. On 24th October, 1993, another member of this gang, Ahmed Mansoor, alias Suhail Ahmed, was also apprehended. He was very close to Anees Ibrahim and his more notorious brother, Dawood Ibrahim. In Delhi, he was the link between Dawood and East West Airlines. Their interrogations, source work and follow-up on information about belonging to a gang and some of the clues quickly gave the CBI a picture of their network. This network had allowed them access to huge funds, protection, shelter and food in Delhi.

The level of their connection again established that, when needed, criminals, indulging in looting and terrorism, had political as well as corporate links to which they turned. We assiduously collected evidence linking Kalpnath Rai, a Congress Minister in the Union Cabinet with independent charge of power, Brij Bhushan Saran Singh, a BJP Member of Parliament and Saboo V. Chacko, the regional manager of the East West Airlines, Delhi — also brother-in-law of Vincent George of the Congress Party, former secretary of Rajiv Gandhi — as their protectors, fund suppliers, shelter providers; call them what you will.

Along with Kalpnath Rai were his secretary, S. P. Rai, who acted as his intermediary. His nephew, V. N. Rai, a suspended Sub Inspector of Police, was also involved as a member of the gang but never apprehended. Another member of the gang, a Sanjay Singh, also eluded arrest. There were 12 who were named in the chargesheet filed in the Special TADA Court of Delhi, presided over by Honourable Special Judge S. N. Dhingra. However, only nine were actually produced. The company, East West Airlines, was named but not physically produced.

Two others, V. N. Rai and Sanjay Singh were prosecuted only as absconders and not produced. East West Airlines was tried and fined ₹50 lakhs for its role in providing funds. Except Brij Bhushan Saran Singh of the BJP, nine persons charged by the CBI were convicted under different sections of the TADA, Arms Act and Conspiracy. They included five persons arrested with arms by the Delhi Police on 23rd July, 1993 and one arrested by the CBI on 24th October, 1993 and those who were their protectors, fund providers, providers of shelter, food and logistics.

They were Kalpnath Rai, S. P. Rai and Sabu V. Chacko. Brij Bhushan Singh was acquitted by Special Judge S. N. Dhingra but we had appealed against his acquittal. To sum up, the punishments by the Special TADA Judge were stiff and fines were steep. After a long drawn trial, examining a large number of witnesses and marking a good number of documents and after questioning each accused under Section 313 of the CrPC and after affording an opportunity to the accused for adducing defence evidence, the TADA Court convicted:

A-1   Subhas Singh Thakore[4] (Also spelt Thakur in different judgements]

A-2   Gyanender Thakore (Also spelt Thakur)

A-3   Shyam Kishore Garikapaty

A-4   Chandrakant Patil

A-5   Paras Mohan Desai

A6   Ahmed Mansoor aka Suhail Ahmed

A-7   Sabu V. Chacko

---

4   *Thakore/Thakur refer to the same persons and are differently spelt in different judgements*

A-8   S. P. Rai

A-9   Kalpnath Rai

A-10   Brij Bhushan Saran Singh was acquitted.

A-12   East West Airlines

A-11   Was an absconder

The first three, Subhas Singh Thakore, Gyanender Thakore and Shyam Kishore Garikapati, were convicted under Section 3(5) and Section 5 of the TADA and also under Section 25 of the Arms Act. Each of them was sentenced to undergo imprisonment for life and a fine of ₹10 lakhs under the first count, imprisonment for five years and a fine of ₹10,000 under the second count, imprisonment for three years and a fine of ₹10,000 under the third count.

- A-4, Chandrakant Patil, was convicted under Section 3(4) and Section 5 of the TADA as well as Section 25 of the Arms Act. He was sentenced to undergo imprisonment for life and a fine of ₹5 lakhs on the first count, imprisonment for five years and a fine of ₹10,000 on the second count and imprisonment for three years and a fine of ₹10,000 on the third count.

- A-5, Paras Mohan Desai, was convicted only under Section 25 of the Arms Act and was sentenced to undergo imprisonment for the period that he had already undergone and to pay a fine of ₹10,000.

- A-6, Ahmed Mansoor, aka Suhail Ahmed, was convicted under Section 3(5) of the TADA and was sentenced to undergo imprisonment for life and to pay a fine of ₹5 lakhs.

- A-7, Sabu V. Chacko, A-8, S. P. Rai, A-9 Kalpnath Rai and A-12, East West Airlines, were convicted under Section 3(4) of the TADA.

- Of them, A-7 was sentenced to imprisonment for five years and to pay a fine of ₹10,000.

- A-8 was sentenced to imprisonment for five years and to pay a fine of ₹500.

- A-9, Kalpnath Rai, was sentenced to undergo prison for 10 years and to pay a fine of ₹10,000 lakhs.

- A-12 was sentenced to pay a fine of ₹50 lakhs, with a period fixed for its payment and provision made for recovery of the fine should in the event of a default in payment by the company.

- A-10, Brij Bhushan Saran Singh, was acquitted by the trial court.

In the Supreme Court, only four, Subhas Singh Thakur, Gyanender Thakur, Syam Kishore Garikapati and Chandrakant Patil, were found fit to be convicted both under the Arms Act and Section 5 of TADA, which provided punishment for those carrying illegal Arms in an area notified under the TADA. Paras Mohan Desai was arrested with a button knife and that was not considered lethal by the Supreme Court for conviction under the Arms Act.

In effect, the conviction was for work done on a single night of 23rd July, 1993 by the Delhi Police. The entire investigation by the CBI officers, evidence to link them with the crimes committed by them before they went into hiding after the serial blasts of 1993 in Mumbai, their staying together in hiding in Delhi, their shelters and all those who provided safe haven to them and provided funds — months of back breaking work by officers and men of the STF and developing sources by STF — became irrelevant for the Supreme Court.

It held, by referring to Article 20(2) of the Constitution of India, that no person shall be convicted of any offence except for violation of a law in force at the time of the commission of the act, it is not enough that one was a member of the terrorist gang before 23rd May, 1993. The Supreme Court further argued that they should have committed a terrorist crime after 23rd May, 1993. Thus the Supreme Court was all for their acquittal.

It declared that those arrested by the Delhi Police on 24th July, 1993 were not members of a terrorist gang. Therefore, their protectors in Delhi too had committed no terrorist crime, the Supreme Court argued. It is embarrassing to state this bluntly but it must be pointed out that this very Court convicted these persons caught together with arms, planning a terrorist act — one is not on an innocent journey, when one carries hand grenades, pistols and knives. By this act of conviction, the Supreme Court also effectively declared them as criminals convicted both under TADA and Arms Act.

Despite their arrest, conviction, past record of being wanted in many crimes including terrorist crimes, their harbourers were acquitted on the ground that from the day — 23rd May, 1993 — this law had come into force, the CBI had produced no evidence that those arrested by the Delhi Police in July 1993 were members of a gang and have committed terrorist acts. The fact that they were gang members and criminals by virtue of their TADA Court conviction was maintained and enhanced by the Supreme Court yet the court closed its eyes to this fact.

The honourable court acquitted their harbourers and funders, Kalpnath Rai, S. P. Rai, Saboo V. Chacko and East West Airlines. Despite the court's own conviction of those they sheltered and funded in Delhi for acts of July 1993, they argued that they were not members of a gang or criminals after 23rd May, 1993! This argument of the Supreme Court is specious and absurd on the face of it. Why specious and absurd? The plain logic of continued membership of a gang member that became a crime under TADA after 23rd May, 1993 escaped their Lordships. Continuing as a gang member is as good as becoming a new gang member.

Further, the judgment was strange and perverse because:

It convicted Subhas Singh Thakore & Co. for their crimes of July 1993.

The Supreme Court accepted the CBI-collected evidence that prior to May 1993 they were Dawood's gang members and had committed terrorist acts as established members of Dawood gang from 1991.

The Supreme Court, by ordering their conviction for their acts in Delhi in July 1993, acknowledged them to be terrorists for acts done after 23rd May, 1993, making them, *ipso facto,* members of a terrorist gang.

They were also awarded punishment for carrying illegal arms on 24th July, 1993, a full two month after the new law was inserted into the TADA.

But, when it came to the CBI's painstakingly-collected evidence showing their terrorist activity as members of Dawood's stormtroopers from 1991, the Lordships stated that the CBI had only produced evidence they were terrorists and members of a gang before 23rd May, 1993. They chose to ignore their own ordered conviction for acts done in July 1993. They used Article 20(2) of the Constitution to free them from the terrorist taint!

The Supreme Court, contrary to the evidence presented, argued that after the insertion of Section 3 (5) of TADA on 23rd May, 1993, there is no evidence showing them as gang members, committing terrorist crime after 23rd May, 1993. The question is how could the Supreme Court take this position?

The court convicted them under both the TADA and Arms Act, for their acts of July, 1993, enhancing their sentences after giving them notice. When they were together in July, 1993, committing a terrorist crime, a full two months after the Section 3 (5) was inserted into the TADA, how could the Supreme Court declare them as non-terrorists, immediately after convicting them as terrorists?

The court further acquitted Kalpnath Rai, S. P. Rai, Saboo V. Chacko and East West Airlines on the ground that giving shelter to those who are not terrorists is not a crime under the TADA. This was one major ground for their acquittal. The Supreme Court also held that prosecution had not established guilty intention *mens rea* against A-7, A-8, A-9 and A-12 in providing shelter to terrorists. The TADA Special Judge believed that it had because the CBI had provided the evidence on *mens rea*. The Supreme Court chose to not even mention it.

What was that material that went unheeded? The guest house shenanigans of Subhas Singh Thakore and Co. were, times without number, brought to the notice of A-8, S. P. Rai and A-9, Kalpnath Rai. They stayed for months paying nothing either for laundry, food, room or any service whatsoever. All their bills were paid on the minister's insistence by the government. The CBI investigating officers' case diary notes how protective the Minister was of S. P. Rai. He himself refused to meet the CBI officers, repeatedly showing his reluctance to face the CBI on the guest house issue.

The case diaries reflect this. Without accepting the premise that A-8, S. P. Rai, was, on his own, dictating terms to the guest house management and notwithstanding the written entries in the guest house register that V. N. Rai, absconder and his associates were guests of the Minister, A-8 was, at least, culpable. Yet, he too was acquitted. The Supreme Court knew that Rai could not order and was aware that personal secretaries are the alter egos of the Minister. Yet, it decided to acquit both! What a travesty of justice!

In Saboo V. Chacko's case, the TADA Judge discussed the evidence of how under Saboo Chacko, East West Airlines had become a huge money laundering operator. He was the kingpin in providing unaccounted money from these operations to Subhas Singh Thakore, Ahmed Mansoor and company. That East West Airlines was a front for the illegal operations of Dawood Ibrahim was a major finding of the TADA Judge. He rightly charged the East West Airlines for harbouring terrorists and fined it ₹50 lakhs, a bare fraction of the ₹9 crores+ that it had illegally amassed for Dawood Ibrahim to further his terrorist operations and other crime syndicate.

The Supreme Court did not discuss this part of the TADA judgement. Instead, its finding was a bland: there was no *mens rea*. The verdict demolished and destroyed a perfectly legal S. N. Dhingra TADA judgement. It allowed the terror-harbouring network in Delhi to continue. In the process, the CBI's anti-terrorist efforts received a major setback and a decent, upright, courageous judge was put to the sword.

It was a monumental error on the face of it. It is a finding that should be declared *non est inventus* (it is not found).

Trashed by a Tribunal

The long arm of the law falls woefully short at times, when the longer arms of extra constitutional authority, using extra constitutional clout — occasionally in the disguise of extreme naivety — take over. How else does the mystery of the Musaliyar & Sons Enterprises (MSE) explain itself? On 7th July, 1995, the Income-Tax Appellate Tribunal overturned separate but identical findings of Assistant Commissioner Income-Tax and the Deputy Commissioner of Income-Tax for two separate assessment years, AY 1991-92 and AY 1992-93, of Musaliyar & Sons.

This was on an original reference from the CBI, holding Musaliyar & Sons Enterprises guilty of grave offences under the Income-Tax Act on 31st January, 1994 and 28th March, 1995 respectively. MSE was located at 2-4B, Silver Apartment, B. Shanker Ghanekar Marg, Dadar West, Bombay: 400028. It was an unregistered firm of Dawood Inc that, the CBI held, had been floated to launder his income from drugs, extortion rackets, murders on payment, cut money from builders and illegal constructions amongst others.

The Tribunal's order, the CBI believed, allowed money extorted over the years through these gruesome crimes to be converted into white money by overturning the two assessment orders. The Special Task Force, the CBI's anti-terrorist unit seized the evidence that MSE, in existence from 1991 to 1993, as a sub-agent of East West Travel & Trade Links (EWTTL) and Nat Travels Private Limited (NTPL) was selling dummy tickets to create cash.

EWTTL — an IATA agent, or NTPL or MSE — was as selling those tickets or merely showing identical sales and ensuring a flow of cash into MSE's coffers. The CBI checked some of the names for itself but not the entire list. EWTTL was also managing East West Airlines, set up in 1982. It was an airline owned by Dawood Ibrahim, as the CBI firmly believed. It also served as a money laundering operator for Dawood & Co.

MSE set up in 1991, with the directors of EWTTL as its partners, was one such operator. The CBI alleged that MSE had laundered something upwards of ₹9 crores between 1991 and 1993. This allegation was taken up for investigation by the tax authority and the later assessment. The findings of the Assessment Officer (AO) of AY 1991-92 are as detailed below:

- The business of EWTTL started in 1982 with a limited staff.
- In 1982, its turnover was ₹30 lakhs.
- In the next 10 years, its turnover increased 100

times. It grew into a ₹350-crore organisation!

- One Nasir Wahid was its non-resident Chairman.

- Thaktiyuddin A. Wahid was its Managing Director (MD)

- Shaibyuddin was the Deputy Managing Director (DMD).

- The work of the international aviation business and taking policy decisions vested with the Chairman. The work of finance, administration, planning, research, marketing devolved upon the MD. The DMD assisted the MD.

- Apart from the management, one Tahiykutty directed all operations from Bombay.

- Its limited staff of 1982 also grew by leaps and bounds. By 1993, it had 28 destinations to look after, with 2,500 employees, apart from 11 substations and 10 aircrafts.

- There was also a cargo division. The management of three had its hands full looking after all operations of EWTTL.

The assessing officer was compelled to conclude thus from his study of the extent of the operations:

> *"Considering the size and growth of the organisation at present, it is clear that the partners (of MSE) who are Directors of EWTTL were very busy. It is also stated that through their excellent marketing strategy that the business substantially increased from 1986 onwards. Not all companies with ₹30 lakhs turnover*

grow 100 times in 10 years, reaching a turnover over ₹350 crores. It is only due to hard work, enterprise, and initiative of the Directors which are responsible for such rare and tremendous growth. Such people are extremely busy and engage themselves in policy making, strategy formulation and planning of the organisation. These areas are vital and has more bearing on the growth of the organisation, whereas clerical and representative jobs are left to the employees. It is therefore beyond imagination that persons of such calibre and brilliance would engage themselves in clerical work like booking tickets (for MSE) which does not involve any challenge and variety which they are capable of taking."

This finding for AY 1991-92 was repeated by the AO assessing AY 1992-93. With this damning material, the finding of both AOs was that MSE collecting upwards of ₹9 crores between 1991 and 1993 could not be true. MSE's claim that it did so with the partners themselves selling tickets was rejected.

One assessing officer noted in his order:

1. MSE did not have a single salaried staff. The claim of the Chairman, MD and DMD of EWTTL was that all clerical work in MSE is done by three of them. This, on the face of it, was absurd.

2. MSE did not have a bank account.

3. MSE did not incur any expenditure on office maintenance, stationery, sundry expenditure and such others.

4.   MSE business was in the service industry but MSE spent nothing on telephone, conveyance and vehicles.

5.   MSE showed receipt of commission of ₹10,000, which was totally disproportionate to what it should have earned.

6.   The claim was that MSE had sold tickets to individuals. The Chairman MD and DMD of EWTTL were all partners in MSE. They claimed all clerical and management work in MSE was shared by three of them.

This claim of selling tickets was checked in a few instances from passengers who had travelled on East West Airlines. They denied having bought tickets from MSE. They bought the tickets from EWTTL and EWTTL duly showed such purchases. The same name appearing in MSE bills was a fraudulent entry, the tax authorities claimed. These persons were contacted and their statement was recorded by the assessing officer.

The finding of the assessing officer (AO) is that:

"The very existence of MSE is not convincing. The whole issue of issuing bills and collecting cash against this bills by partners themselves — who are Directors in EWTTL is far-fetched."

Many questions were asked of the partners, including the fact of their having no infrastructure. The answers were all evasive. Both AOs, after giving opportunities to the partners to contest their findings that MSE existed only on paper and that it was created to facilitate the introduction of unassessed cash into the firm, stood firm on these findings. Both treated the cash with MSE as unexplained cash. Both directed proceedings for recovery and penalty. The CBI reference was, thus, upheld.

The matter then went to the Income-Tax Appellate Tribunal. It was listed before the Judicial Member, KPT Thangali, and Member Vice President, V. Dongzathangi. They set aside both orders. They agreed that MSE had violated Company Law. However, they refused to accept that the cash was unexplained. They argued that MSE was a sub-agent of EWTTL and the price of tickets sold by EWTTL and other agents were passed on to MSE to allow partners buy shares of EWTTL, as they claimed in their defence.

Their argument was that this was the only possible source of this ₹9 crores plus, which is for sale of tickets by EWTTL and other sub-agents, who sold tickets for East West Air Lines. The Tribunal agreed that while this was violative of Company Law, the money was not unexplained cash. It reiterated that the cash could only come from ticketing.

The Tribunal opined that both AOs did not give any finding on how this cash became a part of MSE assets; they did not show the source of the unexplained cash. It was the CBI's firm belief that the unexplained cash was from drugs, protection racket, hush money, payment for murders and such others, which Dawood & Co. ran in

Bombay and elsewhere. It was impossible to produce tangible proof of it.

The CBI did not think it was necessary to show where else the cash could have come from and that the fact of MSE existing only on paper would be adequate proof of ₹9 crores+ with MSE being unexplained cash. Both AOs took this view. They argued that the partners' claim of selling tickets through MSE, which had no existence, no infrastructure, no staff and no bank account, was an absurd argument.

The AO had asked how the Directors of EWTTL could suddenly become clerks in the office of MSE, a sub-agent of EWTTL. In the absence of any believable response, this position was considered untenable and hence the ₹9 crores claimed to have been collected from ticket sale by partners, working as clerks in a non-existing office, from existing people, who denied this claim, was rejected outright. The entire ₹9 crores was held as unexplained cash but the Tribunal argued that the AOs had not established the source of the unexplained cash.

It chose to accept the assessee's position that these were proceeds of sale of tickets by EWTTL and its sub-agents and transferred as loan to the partners of MSE, who were also Directors of EWTTL. They used it to buy shares of EWTTL. The Tribunal conceded that this was not in accordance with Company Law but insisted that the cash of ₹9 crores was not unexplained, insisting further that since the AOs had given no finding on the source of ₹9 crores, it could only be proceeds of sale of tickets by EWTTL and others on whose behalf MSE sold tickets and which they sent to the partners of MSE, who are Directors, virtual owners of EWTTL, so that they could buy shares of EWTTL.

The Tribunal blandly put forth its position with a straight face and allowed the appeal! It did not list all the other points against MSE, which both AOs had raised, as shown above in its findings, nor rebut them. The Tribunal's entire argument was that as the AOs had not explained the source of the ₹9 crores+ and since its only reasoning was that because MSE existed only on paper it was unexplained money, it was unacceptable. The Tribunal held the source was explained by MSE and it accepted that explanation, notwithstanding it being violative of Company Law.

The AOs otherwise well-reasoned order, thus, fell by the wayside, solely on the ground that both orders had no findings on the source of the unexplained cash. Both orders of AY 1991-92 and AY 1992-83 were set aside. A noted CA whom I consulted opined thus:

> *"Additional to income made during assessment on account of unexplained cash are able to sustain in favour of revenue authorities in appellate proceedings only if it is established that real cash got created out of unexplained source. It was necessary to prove that the majority of cash deposit was out of dummy names, who had never travelled or were fictitious sales. Proof of*

creation of own cash or non existence of real business did not get done. The Tribunal in its absence relied on the liability shown to NTPL (the other agent of EWTTL) by MSE and receivables confirmed by EWTTL from NTPL".

In sum, the failure of the income-tax investigating wing to contact each traveller whom MSE showed in its books defeated the CBI and the IT, legally and royally. The question, was it at all necessary in view of the paper existence of MSE, so overwhelmingly proved by both AOs in their separate assessment orders, survives.

The CBI lost the criminal case against those who harboured Dawood's gang members in the Supreme Court and the Income-Tax case of the unexplained cash in the Appellate Tribunal. However, the CBI investigation was upheld in the first instance both in trial Court and at assessment stage in Income-Tax. That was sufficient taxing for the one-time accused of the CBI and Income Tax to end their perfidious operations in the country.

Forces in Friction

The CBI had proved its capability of doing excellent and original work when confronted with terrorism and terrorism-related activities around the 1970s. This was confirmed by its competent handling of the spurt of terrorist activities sparked off by Bhindranwale. It also led to the CBI spawning the National Investigation Agency (NIA).

It needs to be emphasised that none of the terrorist crimes that the CBI prevented and investigated would have been possible without the state governments concerned having consented to a CBI probe. The relief that the CBI intervention provided the states in all terrorist related probes or investigation undertaken laid the grounds for the creation of the NIA.

Yet, today, it would seem like it is a case of the proverbial camel cornering a part of its owner's tent. By an amendment to the NIA Act, many crimes have been brought within the NIA's ambit, necessitating a balanced analysis of the Act itself. The Constitution of India has clearly given primacy to Indian states vis-à-vis the authority to deal with all crimes, including terrorist crimes that occur in their territory. This authority has been surrendered with their having consented to the NIA Act.

This begs the question, what will the Act hold for the states in the long run, now that activities of the so-called "Urban Naxals" are being investigated by the NIA. Other investigations under its ambit are smuggling of high currency and gold, terrorism abroad on Indian assets, violations of international agreements and such others. The non-BJP governed states are ruing their consent to the NIA. So why did they consent?

Corruption within the public services — aided and abetted by those outside the public services — and acts of terrorism are both crimes. The police investigates both. However, having personnel specialised in investigating the corrupt among public services gave the CBI its strength and made for its forte from the time the CBI's first avatar, the Special Police Establishment, was born in 1942.

When did the CBI become a crack force for investigating terrorist crime? Was it with the murder of Deendayal Upadhyaya in 1968 or the murder of the third *Guru* of the Nirankari sect, Gurbachan Singh, in 1980, both of which were investigated by the CBI? Not really, though both were shocking crimes but they were instances of murder.

Deendayal Upadhyaya's murder was by a common railway thief who threw him out of the compartment as it approached the Mughalsarai station, in an attempt to escape the law. As far as the Gurbachan Singh murder was concerned, while it is correct that Ranjit Singh took employment as a carpenter in the Nirankari Mission, intending to assassinate the third *Guru*, he had no personal motive. They were both investigated as cases of murder.

When then was the CBI first assigned the investigation of terrorist crimes? The army action inside the Golden Temple in June 1984, apart from eliminating Bhindranwale and hundreds of his associates, also detained 1,492 persons. Their terrorist role, if any, was the first terrorist related investigation that the CBI was assigned. I was the Chief Investigating Officer (CIO) of this case (See 'CBI Insider Speaks' published by Manas Publications 2015 for details of the investigation).

The government of India then decided that the CBI must continue investigating terrorist crimes that were occurring in the Punjab and elsewhere. Thus was created in 1985-86 a division to exclusively combat terror through investigation. It came to be known as the Punjab Cell. It would be headed by a Deputy Inspector General (DIG) with three Superintendents of Police (S.P.s) with their team of officers reporting to him. I was the first DIG of this division. Swift on the heels of the successful investigation and collection of intelligence on terror crimes first in Punjab and later in Delhi, the states of Haryana and J&K were placed under the ambit of the Punjab Cell.

This work was done along with DIG ranking officers of the states along with the I.B. and RAW officers. The convener of meetings of the officers was the DIG, CBI, Punjab Cell. The meetings were held in Chandigarh, three times a week, for many years. The dossier of information on terror in these states represented yeoman's work to nullify several terror activities in different parts of India. Finding the meeting of minds and sharing on terror useful, three other states, Rajasthan, Gujarat and Maharashtra joined these meetings.

The CBI demanded posts of two more DIGs; one in Chandigarh, to hasten action on receipt of terrorist information and one as DIG (Border), to investigate the influx of aid to terrorists at the borders. The new posts, along with ancillary staff, were quickly sanctioned. The Punjab Cell did excellent work and the government strengthened its sinews. Apart from its successes in Punjab, the Punjab Cell investigated terrorist crimes in Delhi, Maharashtra, Rajasthan and J&K. The states coordinated with the CBI in splendid fashion.

While the lion's share of plaudits must rest with state police personnel and officers of the I.B. and RAW, the Punjab Cell contributed its might to crushing the growth of terrorist activities. When terror resurfaced, following the Babri Masjid desecration in December 1992, I was asked to create an investigation team in my capacity as Joint Director, CBI. This is how the Special Task Force, better known by its acronym, STF, was born. It took over further investigation of the 1993 Bombay Blasts from the Bombay Police as well as the trial of the accused. There were other acts of terrorism in different states that, on the request of the states, the STF investigated.

Thus the CBI remained in anti-terrorist work till the emergence of the National Investigation Agency. The NIA was created by an Act of Parliament in 2008. It became the agency to combat terror in the whole of India. All states and union territories relinquished their first right to investigate terrorist crimes in their territories to the NIA if the agency exercised that option. Even a state that does not give the CBI the right to freely investigate corruption and tempers its consent — which has even gone to the extent of withdrawing consent — gave the NIA complete freedom to operate.

It needs to be emphasised that thus far eight states that had withdrawn consent to CBI investigations have given the NIA complete freedom to operate but only to combat terror. However, since 2019, additional crimes have been added to the NIA's domain expanding its field of operation. This is being perceived by states, especially the non-BJP ones, as violations of the federal *dharma*. This bodes no good as crimes that the NIA deals with need aid and assistance from the law and order agencies of the states.

The CBI Anti-Terrorist investigation received such support to the hilt in Punjab. The then DGP, Julio Ribeiro, the propagator of the "bullet for bullet" motto, wrote on 26th June, 1987 to the Director, CBI with copies to the Union Home Secretary and myself. He wrote:

"I wish to place on record my sincere gratitude to the officers of the CBI who have been entrusted with a difficult job. Shri S. Sen and other officers have worked very hard and with the help of uniformed men raided the various hideouts of the extremists, captured arms and culprits. It will be realised that the gains of the team will also be (to) the advantage of the Punjab Police and all those who are fighting terrorism in the State."

Despite occasional differences in planning operations against terrorists between the uniformed Police and the CBI, there was great co-operation as they worked together. Will the NIA and the state police learn to work in tandem to achieve the best results?

The Stubborn Streak

A Harper Collins publication, An Intent to Serve, the memoires of Tejendra Khanna, a public servant, who last served as Lt Governor Delhi from 2007 to 2013. Khanna had occupied the same post between 1997 and 1998 for a short term, abruptly truncated by the Vajpayee government. The launch of the memoires on 2nd June 2022, at New Delhi's India International Centre, was well attended. The audience included me, for whom the publication had great personal significance.

Tejendra Khanna writes: *"During my first, as well as the subsequent second tenure as LG, Sen (Shantonu Sen) was the principal Raj Niwas Secretariat functionary, assisting me for interaction and follow-up with Delhi Police"*. The Delhi Police is commanded solely by the LG Delhi.

The qualities that he mentions in me in the memoires and those he spoke at the launch set me thinking because it was high praise, indeed. I thought again: was I just being stubborn with my cases? Did this quality, finally, earn me plaudits? So this additional chapter.

Let me recount some incidents and begin from the very beginning. I was six. We lived in Jaipur in a very large mansion. It was a joint family. The matriarch was my 70-year-old grandmother, who reigned supreme. Her five sons, their wives, their children, three widowed daughters and their children lived together. Not always though. Some moved to Kolkata, where we had another house and there they went to college and university. Jaipur was still wanting in higher academic institutions. Even so, throughout the year, about 30 of us lived in Jaipur at a time.

My stubborn streak showed at age six, when my female cousin, four months my senior and I, went roaming over the open spaces in the six-acre compound one winter forenoon. Near the end of the compound, we discovered an old well that was still being operated and we were curious. Every morning and evening, Sukkha, our trusted handyman, hooked a pair of bullocks to a fat rope, one end of which was firmly tethered to a huge leather water carrier. It was lowered over a huge pulley down till it hit the water in the well.

When it was full, Sukkha would sit in between the yoked bullocks and then croon *"Ayoh Jal bhariyouh"* (come let us pull water) and the bullocks would respond. They would run down the path burrowed just for that purpose. Up came the *mashak, the leather water carrier (Hindi: mashak),* bursting and dripping. His junior standing at the top of the well would smartly pull the dripping leather water carrier full of water and steer it on to the mouth of the brick canal and pour it on to its opening.

The canal covered the entire periphery of the house and the extensive outer space that was the green space for flowers, fruits and lawns that surrounded the house. That was also the water supply for all of us in the house. Every morning and evening we would be treated to Sukkha's baritone and loved to hear how his bulls responded.

That forenoon, we escaped all watchful eyes and sneaked to the well. It is still a memory. The long rope hooked to the now dry *mashak* lay invitingly at the bottom of the path that the two bullocks yoked by Sukkha traversed up and down. They brought the water up and, when the task was done, the empty *mashak* lay drying on top of the cemented area that was the mouth of the well. The other rope end lay at a distance. It was tempting. We seized it and pulled. Our action lifted the *mashak* and as it hovered over the empty space of the mouth of the well, becoming heavier, my cousin let go.

The water carrier started going down fast and I, alone, was quite unable to stay its downward move. I would not let go though, even as my cousin pleaded with me. I held on to it but it moved inexorably. I then lay on the soft muddy path made softer by the thudding hooves of the bullock pair and my weight, then 40kgs, stopped it but only for a while. It again started and there I was screaming, fearful but holding on to the rope.

It dragged me, be it ever so slowly, towards the mouth of the well. I did slow it considerably though. By then, my cousin, all of six years four months, finding me determined and unheeding, ran to Sukkha, whose cottage was close by. Sukkha was resting and first thought it was a joke. After all, how could one be dragged and pulled into the well! When he realised that she was serious, he ran to my rescue and finally saved me just five feet from the mouth of the well.

As I think of it now, I would probably not have gone down. At the very end, the rope would have to pull me over the pulley before the plunge down happened. Either it just would not have the momentum or my instinct of self-preservation would have made me let go. Whatever would be, it was my first brush with an "unlawful" authority compelling me to acquiesce to what I thought was wrong and I was not the one to give in.

My elders had neither praise nor understanding for my resistance to the unlawful loss of the *mashak*. I was well and truly punished when the story became public, a fate befalling many who resist unlawful authority!

In school, college and university, I sailed through serenely. I had no occasion to resist authority or be stubborn. Then came service in the CBI. In my early years, I encountered one major resistance to authority. I was regularly attending a trial court in Ahmedabad around 1968-69 in connection with a Birla Textile Mill case. Its top management was accused of certain excise evasions as uncovered during investigations and it was contesting several issues.

I was the Chief Investigating Officer. The Director CBI was Devender Sen, D. Sen, as he was popularly recognised. I was S. Sen. Five ranks separated us. One day I was in his room along with a few others, all senior to me. During our talks, he suddenly turned to me and asked: Why do the Birlas ring you?" I said they do not. He again said they do and this time they called me by mistake. Those days people in my ranks had no official phones and getting a phone connection entailed a 10-year wait. I repeated that they do not and if some Birla or Birla factotum has called him, I will make necessary enquiries. He appeared disinterested in my reply.

Meanwhile, I seethed. The next date in Ahmedabad court was 15 days away. I just walked up to the Birla team and asked them who amongst them had called me in the hiatus and had got through to the Director CBI, who shared my surname. One young lawyer sheepishly said he was on his way to Srinagar and wanted to extend his stay there. He wanted to talk to me to agree to a new date for appearance in court that would get him extra days in Srinagar. Since the person, who he thought was me, turned out to be so gruff and unfriendly, he dropped the whole idea!

The man did not even acknowledge that there was an S. Sen in the CBI, he said. I came back and in two days I just knocked on the Director's door and entered his room. He was surprised. After all, he outranked me by five positions. Our ranks did not go anywhere near him unless called. I stood ramrod after saluting and rattled off what the young lawyer told me. He heard me. His reply was short: "That's all right." I left after saluting him once more. As I stole a glance at him turning to walk to the exit, a good 15 long steps, did I glimpse a tinge of embarrassment? After all, he had denied there was an S.Sen in the CBI!

There came an occasion when the Hon'ble Supreme Court found fault with how the CBI executed the search warrant in our investigation of the Birla Textile Mills, all seven of them, run by G. D. Birla. Our searches were quashed. We listed our what we had seized during the search and returned each document to the several Birla Textile Mills. We had good reason to continue the investigation. There was enough evidence to show malfeasance in the mills' paying central excise duty. This evidence was available from government papers. When a crime had been committed and we had the evidence, the Supreme Court's decision to hold the CBI guilty of not applying the mind while preparing the search warrant was a bit harsh. The mills would in any case be investigated because they had cheated. I wanted the records back. The Birla's were not game, of course, and I was not the one to give up.

After an appropriate interval, I got back the relevant records, just by being stubborn. How was it done? I prepared a detailed affidavit listing the evidence, based on excise returns filed by the textile mill, I was investigating their declaring certain varieties of cloth as coarse when another set of documents by the same textile mills, New Swadeshi and Manjushree Textile Mill, Ahmedabad (hereinafter called mills), filed by it with the office of the Textile Commissioner, Bombay, was seeking an amendment in textile rules to permit them to declare this particular cloth as coarse when under existing textile rules it was fine.

The fine cloth attracted a higher excise tax. While the matter was under correspondence the mill declared the cloth as coarse and paid a lower excise tax. Cheating and conspiracy were writ large. My affidavit pointed this out to their Lordships of the Gujarat High Court. I went on to mention in the affidavit a long list of the mills document, since returned, which had relevance and connection with the criminal charges against the mills. There was one file that, prima facie, indicated that even after the fact of being informed, the top management desired that, though the cloth had not yet been declared coarse by the textile commissioner, the top management directed that excise levy be that as on coarse doth.

It was excise evasion running into lakhs. The Textile Commissioner repeatedly said that the cloth fitted the fine definition and it never gave the mills the waiver they sought. The High Court ordered the mills to submit the records sought to the CBI. The aghast mill lawyers cried foul in a language that clearly annoyed the presiding judge. He admonished them. They appealed. The Supreme Court dismissed it. A suave, yet sheepish Asoke

Sen, then the top Supreme court lawyer, did not lose his cool, unlike the lawyer in Ahmedabad. The mills' top management was duly arraigned before the CBI Special Court, Ahmedabad, in 1975.

There were more to come. The Emergency was at its peak. I had risen in rank and was stationed in Calcutta, in a senior position in the organisation. I faced a situation where, in a criminal investigation, I was directed not to exercise a particular method of investigation against a particular class of people. It is the infamous fiat of Vidya Charan Shukla, then Minister of State for Home, the poster boy of the Emergency. No company under investigation could be searched under the criminal procedure code, which was an illegal order. But it was the Emergency and who would dare question?

A Deputy Commissioner of Central Excise showed favour to a well-known tobacco company and, in the process, obtained substantial amounts to finance a magazine that he privately published. The order to investigate the Deputy Commissioner, Central Excise, Calcutta came with the specific direction that the tobacco company was not to be searched during the investigation. It was an illegal order but how could I ignore it?

I decided to undertake an operation that was not a search but it would look like a search. The day the Deputy Commissioner was searched in his office and residence, I sent a team to the tobacco company with a list of documents that I wanted them to trace immediately and hand over to my officers in the presence of two independent witnesses. The tobacco company rang up Vidya Charan Shukla. He, in his turn, spoke to Director CBI. Within the hour I was called by Director. He wanted an explanation. I was ready. I was not conducting any search, I told him.

Why then had I sent a team and why witnesses? I said that the list was long and my officers would be required to check the record for its relevance. The witnesses were present to testify that we only asked them to produce the documents. He heard me out quietly. Much to my surprise, not once did he lose his cool with me. Instead, on his own, he said that this tobacco company was a member of the Tobacco Council of India and the Minister of State for Home, Vidya Charan Shukla, had asked him about the CBI team on the premises of the tobacco company.

The Director, a veteran in the game, asked me what if they wanted some time to produce the documents? Would I give them time? I understood there was a limit to my stubbornness when I worked in a hierarchical organisation. In the very next hour, the tobacco company asked for time and I withdrew my men. Other battles lasted longer.

It was in the sweltering heat of June 1984, that the Army Operation to oust and eliminate Jarnail Singh Bhindranwale and his band of outlaws from the Golden Temple Complex, Amritsar, was mounted. It lasted longer than the Army anticipated. At the end of it, the CBI was directed to investigate the role of the 1492 who were detained by the Army. I headed a large team of CBI officers to do this.

The Army heads, the Defence Minister (K. P. Singh Deo) and my chiefs were convinced that the apprehension of 1492 during the Blue Star Operation was sufficient ground to prosecute them under the stringent provisions of the Indian Penal Code and existing terrorist laws, whereby the punishment included death. As Chief Investigating Officer, I and my team worked to find hard evidence against the detained 1492.

Finally, evidence to charge only 379 of them emerged in my book. Those who still maintained that mere detention by the Army was evidence enough did not have their way. They our-ranked me and were determined but it was evidence and proof that had its way. I resisted them, and had my way. I made some people angry.

There is a footnote though. It came in the July 1985 Rajiv-Longowal accord, a little more than a year after their detention by the Army, whereafter all 379 were set at liberty. I witnessed the welcome they got; how they were received by Siddhartha Shankar Ray, Governor of Punjab. Of the hard-core terrorists, about 250 of them were killed in the operation. My stubbornness prevented the hapless pilgrims and worshippers, nearly 1,100 of them, caught in the crossfire, from being held in the Jodhpur Jail. This was a jail built to detain terrorists.

After this investigation CBI, hitherto an Anti Corruption body, which also investigated a few economic crimes was thrust into investigating terrorist crimes. What was popular as a band of CBI men known within the CBI as Punjab Cell, was named a Special Investigating Unit with three Superintendents of Police, headed by a Deputy Inspector General of Police (DIG) who reported to the Director CBI.

I was its first DIG. We started our work in 1985 and a series of terrorist incidents were successfully investigated. These included the murder of Gen A. S. Vaidya in Pune in 1986; the Ludhiana PNB dacoity of suspected 7 million in 1987; the Manchanda murder of 1987 and the Syed Modi murder in 1988 to name a few. There were a few more but one incident merits more than a mention.

It related to one *Pracharak (in India) a person appointed to propagate a cause through personal contact, meetings, public lectures, etc* of the Dam Dami Taksaal (name withheld). He was wanted for seditious speeches and preaching violence. He was finally caught in Muktsar. Since road travel during those days in the Punjab often led to encounters, I arranged to bring him to Delhi in a BSF helicopter. The Director, CBI, (M. G. Katre) received a call from the Minister of Stare Internal Security (Arun Nehru) suggesting that be brought to Delhi by road. When I heard it, I objected and when I was overruled, I planned to lead the team of CBI officers from Delhi to Muktsar with a force armed to the teeth.

The Director did not like the idea of me being a member of the escort team. I was adamant as I feared the decision of not allowing a helicopter, which I had arranged for, was inviting a serious mishap. There was every chance of a fatal incident as was happening often in the Punjab. I did not want it to happen under my charge.

There was a very annoyed Director, on the one hand, his Minister on the other but it was his DIG who, finally, forcefully intervened. The plans were changed and the arrested preacher was flown into Delhi. I am convinced that I saved his life.

The next instance was the case of importing Czech pistols, the complete details of which elude me after so many years. I do remember though that there was a scandal. The Ministry of Home Affairs was a party and wanted an investigation. The import of Czech pistols by the Home Ministry raised a stink in the nineties. One wanted person took refuge in the U. K. He did not wish to be described as an absconder. He lived in upscale Shantiniketan in South Delhi and while he responded to our notice, he sought to delay his questioning by seeking the Delhi High Court's intervention.

He engaged the very best lawyers to suggest he was not into any crime. He lost because we had done our homework. He was directed to appear before CBI by a specific date. We had made it clear that his would be a custodial interrogation. A day or two before he was to land, our plans to arrest him were complete. At this time the Director (MG. Katre) directed the Chief Investigation

Officer, an SP, not to arrest him. He was reportedly too sick.

I was informed by the SP, who reported to me, that the Director's order overruled mine. I directed him to convey the Director's verbal orders to me by putting it into words. He did so. At once I recorded a note to the effect that the CBI is committed to arresting him as he lands. We had told the Delhi High Court that he would be subjected to custodial interrogation. Within the hour. the Director was on the RAX (a phone restricted between 400 officers of GOI) and said the Home Minister (Buta Singh) did not want him to be arrested.

He added, for good measure, that he appreciated my point and that I could proceed as I had planned. He faced the upset Home Minister. Neither was pleased with me. I had my way. I ordered his arrest and we did. Those were halcyon days of the CBI for me. Decisions that went against the superior's expressed desires, wishes and orders, call them what you wish, were never easy but if taken and explained, howsoever contrary to their orders, one could survive in the department with honour. I did.

This did not last, however. With the arrival of a Director in 1993, things radically changed. He was Prime Minister Narasimha Rao's nominee though he, Vijay Rama Rao, had never worked with the CBI. I was then Joint Director CBI for two years, with both the anti-corruption central units and the Eastern anti corruption units of the CBI in Kolkata, Patna, Dhanbad,

Bhubaneshwar and Ranchi reporting to me. Plus, I had an additional charge for creating a team that would eventually investigate and prosecute the 1993 serial Bombay Bomb Blast.

From the beginning, my body language upset him. He had no idea of the CBI units and how they functioned. The time-honoured CBI standard of no misuse of the staff car was never honoured by him. He did not have a car of his own. Frankly, I did not find in him qualities of a CBI Director. Probably, I showed it. He did not like me either, though my unit did an excellent job.

Some instances are exemplary: in collecting evidence; arresting an additional nine people who had escaped the dragnet of Bombay police during the 1993 Bombay Blast investigation; in collecting substantial evidence to link Pakistan ISI with Dawood's machinations behind the serial 1993 Bomb Blasts; in collecting material to solve the more than 40 IED explosions in Bombay that were unsolved; in solving the case of the train blasts in all five premier trains on the anniversary of Bahri Masjid demolition on December 6. 1993, linking them to Dr Jalees Ansari, all done within a fortnight of the investigation being transferred to the CBI by the states where the crime occurred.

Vijay Rama Rao just did not like me. Gone were the days when the Director of CBI did not take amiss his subordinates challenging a direction. Not only they did not take it amiss, D. Sen (1968-1975) and those that followed him, Messrs C. V Narasimhan, (the topper and stickler for rules) John Lobo (the tallest stalwart of all), J. S. Bawa (the most big-hearted), M. G. Katre (the great professional), R. Sekhar (honest and simple; bereft of show and pomp) and S. K. Dutta (without a mean bone in him), all much-admired, who rose to the Director's position after working in the CBI in other ranks, who stood up and defended me and others like me when our legal actions went against the interest of powerful elements who had access to politicians who were powerful Ministers.

Vijay Rama Rao brought me down step by step. He asked me about my heavy charge one day. I admitted it was heavy. He soon relieved me of my main charge and asked me to deal only with the 1993 Bomb Blast. It could have been otherwise. It was one of the prized charges and I had earned it by sheer merit. He wanted a man he could control.

Mercifully, I retired in a year's time without fanfare. In that year though, I faced several attacks and challenges under Vijay Rama Rao's tenure. A matter of rent is interesting. During the time of Director, R. Sekhar, who preceded him and two Directors before him my recently constructed house was sought for the newly-created office of DIG CBI, Jaipur. All procedural steps were taken and, after the Director's approval, I gave it on a monthly rent of 4,500/ per month. Incidentally, the CPWD assessment was 7,500/ per month but the Director CBI's power was limited to 5,000/ per month.

Vijay Rama Rao was informed, obviously he wanted to know how to fix me that the CVC had asked the CBI to enquire into this deal. The enquiry had taken place during the time of R. Sekhar's successor, Vijay Karan. No fault was found in the process. This I learnt from S. K. Dutta, who was Vijay Rama Rao's immediate predecessor. Vijay Rama Rao reopened the case and issued a formal warning letter to me; my only official reprimand in my entire career in the CBI.

His ground? He wrote that since I was a CBI officer, he construed that I had official dealings with CBI. Under conduct rules, I was required to take Director CBI's prior permission before negotiating to rent my house to anyone with whom I had official dealings. This, I had nor done, prior to submitting the proposal to the then Director CBI, R. Sekhar! He sought no explanation from me for this alleged violation of conduct rules. He blocked all chances of my securing post-retirement jobs, whether it was in the Ministry of Health or Interpol Paris, from where I had definite offers. He continued his animus against me post-retirement.

After retirement, I was offered a consultancy under the Ministry of Chemicals. This was to look into why the National Fertilizer Corporation had failed to import even one gram of urea after paying in advance ₹ 133 crores to a Turkish company. This consultancy was also terminated at his instance after I named the Prime Minister's son, Prabhakar Rao, as a person of interest in the Urea scam. Subsequently, there was a possibility of joining as Managing Director, Vigilance, in the General Insurance Corporation (GIC), which was spiked by the CVC, N. Vittal, no doubt on his advice.

D. Sengupta, Chairman GIC told me that the CVC's comments on my file were: "I have reservations about Sen." I had an outstanding record. I stood decorated with the Indian Police Medal for Meritorious Service and the President Police Medal for Distinguished Service. True, I had not helped my cause. I had recommended the investigation of the PM's son, Prabhakar Rao and also questioned the role of the Secretary to the PM, the Cabinet Secretary himself and the Revenue Secretary in the matter of the ₹ 133 crores lost in the urea deal by the National Fertilizer Corporation. I had made too many enemies.

My stubborn streak, I do not regret. More so, when I read the memoires: An *officer that I invited to join the Raj Niwas team was Shantonu Sen, who had retired as Joint Director Central Bureau of Investigation (CBI) in April 1996, a few months before my own superannuation. Sen carried a reputation as a highly competent, honest and uncompromising professional whom I happened to meet in the Commerce Ministry when he was looking into the NFL fertiliser import scam. His ability to sift the grain from the chaff was both remarkable and unassailable. During my first, as well as the subsequent second tenure as LG, Sen was the principal Raj Niwas Secretariat functionary, assisting me for interaction and follow up with Delhi Police."*

My stubbornness was lost on Vijay Rama Rao, N. Vittal and several others. It earned me dividends from all Directors before Vijay Rama Rao and all Central Vigilance Commissioners before N. Vittal. From Tejendra Khanna, I received this thumping endorsement and I am content and hold that our stubborn streak to uphold the law is our strength; not our weakness. He backed me when both Home Minister P. C. Chidambaram and Chief Minister Sheila Dikshit wanted me out for reasons that he has never shared with me.

Two Doctor Terrorists

One is Ayman Al- Zawahiri dob 19-06-1951, an Egyptian from Cairo. The other is Jalees Ansari, dob 01- 07-1952, Indian from Mumbai. Zawahiri was 71 when he succumbed to drone killing in a Kabul safe house and Jalees is 70 today serving a life sentence, in Jail, from January 1994 They are recognised terrorist names. They have similarities. Ayman and Jalees became doctors in the 80s. They drifted into terrorism as students and interns. The "infidel" regime in Egypt and a visit to the Afghan war zone provided the ammunition to fuel the terrorist fire in young Ayman then just eighteen. As a young doctor of a Cairo clinic he found himself treating Islamic forces fighting the Soviet forces in Afghanistan. Jalees too started young. Hailing from district Basti in Uttar Pradesh the Ansari family moved to Maharashtra.

Jalees was born in then Bombay. He studied in Dr Ahmed Sailor School Boiwada and then in Maharashtra College before entering BVT Hospital Sion for his MBBS degree in 1972. However, he suffered from schizophrenia and had to take a break. He got his MBBS degree, finally, in 1981 from Lokmanya Tilak Medical College. It was in the medical college years that he faced jibes, taunts and racial attacks and he attributes his communal bent of mind to them. He claims not only students also teachers were a part of the taunts and insults group. He lived in Moomin pura Agripada Bombay 400011 where the majority were Muslims. His communal mind was further aggravated by the horrific stories of Nellie Communal killings in Assam and Bhiwandi Communal Riots in Maharashtra. Around the same time his masjid in Moomin pura was visited by two rabid speakers who roused communal passions fever pitch. They were identified during investigation. One was Azim Gauri and the other was Abou Masund They belonged to Hyderabad and Kolkata West Bengal respectively. When on 6th December Babri Masjid was demolished he saw in this act the confirmation that the cause he espoused was right.

He created a group which he named "Tanzeem Ishlahul Musalmeen". They, to start with, comprised youngsters of Moominpura who ostensibly were together to fulfill social needs of people in who lived in Moominpura. Simultaneously he created a inner core of like minded people. Subversive action was their primary objective. This group was, initially, of 8/10 people. It expanded, exponentially, unknown to Maharashtra intelligence and Mumbai police.

While Ayman Al Zawahiri was with Al-Queda planning terrorism internationally his co- religionist and also a doctor like him was executing terrorist acts with in India. He started his terrorist activity in 1990 and his career ended in early 1994 at the hands of Special Task Force CBI which was created in 1993. Under Al Zawihiri's leadership, and he was crucial to the Al- Queda network, Al- Queda carried out the deadliest attack ever on American soil, the September 11 2001. Earlier, he had executed terrorist attacks in 1998 in American Embassies in Tanzania and Nigeria. He reshaped the organisation from a centralised planner of attacks into the head of a franchise chain. He led the creation of network of autonomous branches around the regions in the Middle East in Iraq, Saudi Arabia, Yemen. in Africa including North Africa and Somalia. He was targeting India when he was killed by a U S drone strike in Afghanistan on 31st July 2022. Dr Mohammad Jalees Ansari in India from mid-eighties was actively organising his terrorist aims. His fervour and zeal brought existing ISI trained militants from Kashmir and elsewhere flocking to him. He obtained passports from Lucknow and Mumbai. He had three of them. He travelled, enlarged and expanded. He was helped with money and material to expand. His first known terrorist activity was in Malegaon in District Nasik in 1990.

He was arrested by Nasik Police. In Crime no 65/90 of Police Station Kilia Malegaon. He was in custody under section 4 & 9 of the Explosive Substances Act 1908. The investigation was poorly done and not only he was bailed out he also was forgotten. Emboldened and armed with men, money, materials. supported by ISI

Pakistan and like-minded in India he let loose his terror apparatus. From 1990 to 1993 his men and he himself planted Improvised Explosive Devices (IED) in 53 places. Mostly, in Maharashtra, a few in Andhra, Karnataka, 25 of them in Mumbai itself. There was substantial damage to property and infrastructure. No lives were lost but he created fear in the majority community. He earned, in his circle, a reputation as a master in tactical terrorism as neither he nor his associates were apprehended. Many Police Stations in Maharashtra took up the challenge to apprehend him. Like, Borivali Police Station in crime no 80/90, Kurla Police Station in Crime no 490/91 Mahim Police Station under Crime no 76/92 and failed. More and more police stations were targeted by him. Not one of the 53 blasts were solved. He was confident that his planning and execution was fool proof. It was then that he launched his blitzkrieg.

Six explosions on six prestigious trains on 6th December 1993. His master plan. The Babri Masjid demolition of 6th December 1992 was to be avenged in this manner. His planning was successfully executed. At 10.50 pm on 5th December 1993, a bomb went off on the Rajdhani Express enroute from New Delhi to Howrah when the train was near Kanpur Railway Station in Uttar Pradesh. The next day at 5 am there was another blast on the Rajdhani Express on its way from Howrah to New Delhi, again near Kanpur. At 5.15 am, there was another blast, once again on the Rajdhani Express going from Mumbai Central to New Delhi near Kota railway station in Rajasthan. At 6 am, the fourth bomb went off on the Flying Queen Express going from Surat to Mumbai at Bestan railway station in Valsad, Gujarat. The fifth bomb blast took place at 7.05 am on the Andhra Pradesh Express from Hyderabad to Nizamuddin near Malkajgiri in Andhra Pradesh. The sixth was set for Bangalore- Kurla Express but it was thwarted as the explosive device was detected and thrown out of the train near Karjat in Maharashtra.

The investigation was taken up in by the nearest police station in the state where the explosion took place. For three weeks there was no break-through. These explosives though improvised had caused injuries and deaths on the trains. That fatalities were less was just luck.

The Special Task Force with in CBI which reported to me, on the orders of the Government of India and with the concurrence of States where the train blasts were under investigation, took over further investigation in all six incidents on 28/12/93. We got down speedily and with alacrity. I immediately took stock of all the developments in each case. Hyderabad police only, by then had some clues. DIG S TF Neeraj Kumar immediately proceeded to join Hyderabad police and work on the clues. I proceeded to Bombay and joined the Bombay Unit of the STF. which had commenced investigation of the crime. The story of undetected IED exploding all over Maharashtra including 25 in Mumbai was material seeking a break through. On my direction police stations in Maharashtra dug deep into the case history of all blasts since 1990. From early hours in the first week of January ours and theirs ceaseless effort was to find any clue that could link any one involved in any one of the blasts in Maharashtra with the train blast cases. It was work day and night. The break came on in early second week January 1994 when Malegaon Police from PS Killa reported the arrest in 1990 and subsequent bail of Mohamed Jalees Ansari in its Crime No 65/90 in their yet (Jan 1994) unsolved case under the Explosive Substances Act. Neeraj Kumar from Hyderabad also informed me that one Jalees Ansari of Moominpura has emerged as a prime suspect. I lost no time in mounting a 24/07 surveillance operation on him. The first team comprising non-Muslims officers made no headway. They though in plain clothes and in disguise reported hostility, lack of co-operation.

I changed the team to all Muslim men and officers. This team of Muslim men and officers of CBI and Bombay had dug out enough material on Dr Mohamed Jalees Ansari to enable me to direct Superintendent (SP) S T F Bombay CBI Satish Jha to search his house in Moominpura. This search was carried out in the early hours of 13/01/94. It yielded rich dividend. He was present in the house and he and his group, even some neighbour stoutly resisted the operations. It required the SP both tact, authority and courage to carry on the search operations. At his place tools of crime found were explosives, weapons of foreign make (Beretta 9 mm Pistol, Webley Scott. 38 Revolver, & Smith and Wesson. 38 revolver), country made revolvers, ammunition, foreign currency, Indian currency (2.59 lac) instruction manual for preparing and using explosives, wireless sets, detonators, timing devices, choppers and knives. His arrest and interrogation revealed his country wide network. Five of his associates were immediately traced and arrested. Dr. Ansari bubbling with zeal and fervour after his train blasts was getting ready with his plans for more terrible strikes on 15th January in Bombay and 26th January in Delhi His arrest prevented them

All the six incidents were clubbed as one conspiracy by CBI. One blast in and around Kota in Rajasthan could be tried in Ajmer (Rajasthan). I choose this court for the trial of all the conspirators. For one Ajmer was in Rajasthan. I had served as DIG, CBI Jaipur. The Rajasthan police judiciary in all ranks, had a well-earned reputation of being responsive and efficient. Plus being a Jaipurian, myself, I had lot of personal rapport in the State and Ajmer was close to Delhi. The trial commenced in the Special Court at Ajmer in 1994. The accused were charged with terrorist Crimes as well as under sections of the Indian penal code and under Explosive Substances Act. At the end of the investigation, he and twenty others were linked to the six cases First sixteen were arrested early. The kingpin Jalees and his five associates were arrested on 13th and 14th January and ten of them were subsequently arrested. Five absconded. Rewards were announced and efforts yielded results. The remaining five were also traced and arrested. The trial continued till 2004 and all 21 were convicted on 28/02/2004 with Dr

Jalees Ansari sentenced to life imprisonment after a trial lasting ten years in Ajmer.

The conviction was maintained by the Supreme Court on May 11, 2016. The Supreme Court judgement was written by Justice Uday U Lalit, who was later the 49th CJI. They are serving their sentence as of date.

It's ironical that while we chose law to put away Jalees and the Americans chose a drone we both took about the same time. We in 2016 for crimes committed between 1990-1993 and they in 2022 for crimes committed between 1998-2001.

One last word. Terrorists can well be eliminated through the barrel of a gun. Through law it's more fitting, more thorough and more devastating.

Political Bullies

You meet them in civil service. You encounter them at work. They can be, and often are, nasty. They confront you when you think that you are a big shot yourself! In hindsight, they make for interesting raconteuring.

Let me number them and then describe my innings with them.

Bully No. 1

The one that scored

He was the newly-appointed Governor of a newly-made Indian state, where I was on loan from the CBI. I was the Anti-Corruption chief and quite the authority, or so I thought! I had a lovely cottage, with a spacious lawn where every morning, when the sun was out, the Kanchenjunga too was out, shimmering and shining. This cottage stood tall in the Governor's Estate. Protocol demanded that I call on him. I did. He was formal as was expected. I was already two years on. So glibly and coherently, I explained my job and I thought my one-to-one meetings with His Excellency had ended.

But no. He wanted to meet me more often. He wanted details of my work. My boss was the Home Secretary. He clearly did not wish me to visit the Raj Bhawan and rightly so. That was his beat. He was a Bhutia and a 'noble' of the erstwhile kingdom. He and I agreed that His Excellency and I should not meet to discuss my work. When I politely did tell him that, he did not like it. He bullied me to give in but failed to break my resolve. To cut a long story short, after a few months, he got me to vacate the cottage. Then the Government of India cut short my tenure. He had resolved to send me out and back to the CBI.

There lay the rub.

Here I was on a higher rank, with higher pay and three children in school, whose sessions differed from sessions in Delhi. I wanted two tenures. He cut short even my first one. The Chief Minister, however, was very appreciative of what I had done and was keen that I should continue. The Governor was not one to remain idle. The PM of India was related to him. Her late husband was some sort of a cousin of his. I learnt from the Home Secretary, India, that the PM's ears were poisoned well and truly against me.

This, I learnt when the Chief Minister sent me on an official trip to Delhi to plead my own case. The Chief Minister also sent the State Establishment Secretary to Delhi. The Finance Minister of the state was already in Delhi, got time from the PM and took him to see her.

She was all ears, all smiles and asked her sidekick, the one who went by the acronym RKD, to take notes. The Establishment Secretary told me that he saw RKD take out his near-empty cigarette packet on which he took notes! As they left, the Establishment Secretary saw him from the corner of his eyes, taking out the remaining cigarette and throwing the packet into the dustbin, note and all.

I realised the game was over, for me. I took four months' leave, salary in hard cash, got a fabulous farewell, a great escort and returned to the Government of India. I had a very difficult two years before I got promoted. I lost a lot of money and suffered position-wise as well. That is Bully no. 1.

There were more.

Bully No. 2

By hook or by...

The first Bully lost his job after 1984, when his support, the PM, was tragically gunned down on October 31, 1984. However, the PM had never gone after me.

The second bully became Prime Minister in 1989. It was 1988 when, as DIG CBI Punjab Cell, we chargesheeted Sanjay Singh along with others for the murder of Syed Modi. We thought it was an airtight case. This Sanjay Singh was a politician. For years he was in the Congress. Thus, during investigations, when the Congress was in power, P. Chidambram, India's Internal

Security Minister, told the CBI Additional Director, who was temporarily heading the CBI (since the Director CBI, M.G. Katre was abroad) that Sen should not investigate Sanjay. When he asked me to lay off, I gave reasons why it was necessary to investigate Sanjay Singh. When the Director CBI returned, he asked me and heard from me the why it was necessary to investigate Sanjay Singh. The Minister was then told that as Sen was in charge of the investigation and on the spot, he would investigate on his terms if he continued to be in charge of the investigation. Further, sitting in Delhi, they told the minister, he could not tell Sen whom to investigate and whom not to. However, Sen could be removed along with his team if the Minister so wanted. The Minister stopped short there and did not press for this solution but was annoyed.

I made a permanent foe of him, though. Years later, between 2007 and 2013, when he was for some time, the Home Minister of India, and I was the OSD to the LG Delhi, he repeatedly told him that as a retired officer and nearing 70, I should be replaced. My Lt Governor chose to ignore his suggestion.

The bully in my books was Sanjay Singh's uncle-in-law who became India's Prime Minister (1989-1990). His joint secretary, one Bhure Lal, asked the Director CBI, Rajendra Sekhar, to remove the ace public prosecutor, whom the CBI had specially selected and appointed to prosecute those chargesheeted for the murder of Syed Modi. S.K. Dutta, once my very senior colleague in the Kolkata CBI, and then CBI no. 2, gave me this account.

It appears that the Director CBI Rajender Shekhar asked him to accompany him to Prime Minister's Office, (PMO) and told Bhure Lal Joint Secretary PMO In his (Dutta's) presence that he and his no. 2 would surrender their uniforms rather than remove the Special Public Prosecutor, Desai.

The bully that he was, the Prime Minister, removed all prosecutors appointed in all departments of the Government of India in one stroke. Every department lost its prosecutor. We too lost Desai.

V.P. Singh lost his job in 1990 but, to me, he will remain a political bully.

He also placed a new trial judge, who discharged Sanjay and his paramour, Ameeta Modi, wife of the slain Syed Modi. Four months later, the trial Judge was made a judge in the Allahabad High Court, bench Lucknow.

Bully No. 3

Just deserts

This one was the criminal himself. He was a Cabinet-Minister in the P.V. Narasimha Rao (1991-1996) Cabinet; as the Minister of State Minister for Power (Independent Charge) no less. I got the better of him thanks to a stern and upright Special CBI Judge in the Delhi Karkardoma Court.

The story briefly runs thus. The CBI, Special Task Force (STF), which I headed as the Joint Director, was required to complete the 1993 Bombay Blast investigation, taking charge of the incomplete chargesheet of the Bombay Police. The STF was spreading a dragnet for Dawood Ibrahim's goons. They were running for cover. The STF and the police of many states, in close coordination, were in hot pursuit.

On July 23, 1993, the Delhi Police apprehended five of them in Delhi in two Toyota cars at 4 am in the morning in the Red Fort area. They were carrying arms – pistols, hand grenades button knives. They had been hiding in Delhi for a few months. On July 27, 1993, the Government of India ordered the STF to take over the investigation from the Delhi Police. The STF was tasked to find who gave them shelter, food, finances and logistical support and also to trace and apprehend others.

To cut a long story short, among their financiers, protectors and providers of logistical support, we zeroed in on this Cabinet Minister (Kalpnath Rai) and others. To name just a couple, Saboo V. Chacko, Regional Manager, East West Air Lines and Brij Bhushan Sharan Singh, a BJP MP. The Minister defied our investigation attempts.

Kalpnath Rai had ordered the National Thermal Power Corporation to put them up and treat them as guests. They were feasted and feted at the tax-payer's expense. The East West Air Lines Regional Manager provided them, on orders of Dawood, who owned the airlines, the finances that they needed to live in Delhi. Chacko was the Regional Manager and also the brother-in-law of Vincent George, former sidekick of Rajiv Gandhi.

To go back to the bully, Kalpnath Rai, he refused to meet the investigating officers to answer the criminal charges that the STF had raised against his doings to shelter Dawood's goons. He abused the officers. Since the CBI does not charge the person proposed to be chargesheeted without ascertaining the defence, I ordered a chargesheet against all accused who had given their defence and we had enough evidence to rebut them. On Kalpnath Rai, I ordered that they tell the court that while there were charges but not having his defence, "investigation continues". I had anticipated that our fearless Judge (Dhingra) might just order that the evidence was sufficient to chargesheet him to arrest and produce him. This happened. He so ordered.

The DIG STF, Neeraj Kumar (later Commissioner of Police, Delhi) and his team were a part of the STF. On my orders, he entered the serving Cabinet Minister's bungalow in Lutyens Delhi at 10 pm. He was arrested. He was interrogated for part of the night. Absolute secrecy of the operation was ensured. The Director CBI was very disturbed by the state of affairs as it was. No publicity was to be given to the arrest by the media, my Director had cautioned me. I ensured that. The next morning, before 10 am, he was produced before Judge Dhingra, whom I had requested to hold his court 10 minutes before his usual schedule, which was 10 am. In a few minutes, he was sent to judicial custody/remand. This is how publicity was minimised.

Along with others, he remained in jail during trial. He was convicted by Judge Dhingra along with 10 others and sentenced to 10 years imprisonment and fined ₹10 lakhs

True, later, on appeal after years of incarceration, the Supreme Court held, that all except those arrested by Delhi police on 23rd July were not guilty of terrorism. The law that made them terrorist did not apply to them as when they were harbouring. financing and protecting terrorist the law was not in force! It was an order without precedent. The Indian Penal Code (IPC) section for harboring criminals was also forgotten! It was a bizzare order.

Bully No. 4

Clean bowled

This time, I lost my right to take the investigations to their right full conclusion, lock stock and barrel. Not one but two ongoing investigations. They were mega crimes and the criminals were in the top rungs. The bully was powerful and so were his accomplices. They hurt me and, though I fought right back, I could do little. I suffered in service till I retired. They blocked the post-retirement jobs that were offered to me in the public sector. These were taken away.

Let me here, say that powerful people under investigation use power to fend it off and the crime busters in the CBI have a duty to counter them. I did it as I swore by CBI motto INDUSTRY IMPARTIALITY INTEGTITY.

In 1992, as Joint Director CBI Anti-Corruption, two crimes needed my best efforts. One involved investigating the Jain Havala Diary and the other corruption by a highly-rated hero of the public sector, Venkataraman Krishnamurthy. [Details are extensively reported in my book CBI Insider Speaks (Truth of the Havala Scam and Krishnamoorthy Saga) and also in Foul Play by Shiv Vishwanathan and Harsh Sethi (Hero of the Public Sector) Story of V. Krishnamurthy. Both investigations were first taken away from my charge when, in 1993, I was divested of my charge as the Joint Director Anti-Corruption, CBI by the Director CBI. Both cases have been explained in detail in the two books mentioned. They are cases of horrendous corruptions. Both these crimes, if only they were taken to their logical end!!

As a result of my efforts to take them to their logical end, I suffered at the hands of the Director CBI (1994-1996). He blocked my attachment as Director Intelligence, Ministry of Health as a personal selection of the Health Minister, A.R. Antulay. He refused to get the Government of India to agree to my deputation to Interpol Lyons, France, a position that I had obtained while in service on an application through the proper channel. He also, declined my request – after an assurance from the Joint Secretary, Ministry of Personnel, that having completed two years as Joint Director, I had a genuine case to be considered for a higher rank – to forward my case for a higher appointment, for which I had become eligible after completing two years as Joint Director, CBI. I was in this rank from January 1992 to April 1996, without any promotion. The bully and his accomplices had tossed me to Timbuktoo.

But fate was not done with me yet. The bully / lies again crossed my path. It happened thus. I retired on April 30, 1996, at 58 years of age. Immediately thereafter, the Secretary Chemicals, Indrajit Chaudhury, IAS, a friend from my Hindu College, Delhi, days rang me up. He had an assignment for me. A public sector enterprise in his Ministry, the National Fertilizer Corporation (NFL) had been cheated to the tune of $38 million or ₹133 crores by a Turkish company. This later became the infamous urea scam. ₹133 crores had been paid in advance for 200,000 metric tons of urea, remitted through the SBI, with not a gram of urea delivered! The CBI was sitting on the Complaint of the NFL.

The CBI had to investigate who was responsible. This was my task. Foul Play, a Seminar publication 1998; CBI Insider Speaks, Manas Publication 2015 and Corruption, CBI and I, Authors Upfront, published in 2020, carry details of this notorious case; beginning, climax and end.

In a nutshell, I established that it was a conspiracy in which the NFL officials were catspaws to the big fish in the Government and private persons, who comprised close relatives and included the favourite son of the former Prime Minister of India (1991-1996). They were members of the conspiracy. The Parliamentary Committee on Chemicals under the Chairmanship of A.R. Antulay also reached the same conclusion. It is another story that the report was never tabled. A.R. Antulay gave me a copy but said he could not table it. ELECTIONS HAD BEEN ANNOUNCED

I gave it to the then Editor of The Statesman, Delhi.

I had studied the conspiracy angle.

A comprehensive complaint was again prepared, naming the possible conspirators as well as the dubious Turkish company. It was despatched to the CBI by the MD of NFL on my suggestion. For a month, no action was taken, presumably, because the non official accused were all "Raos" and the CBI Director, well briefed earlier was even more reluctant.

How did I get the investigation to move? Remember the 13-day Vajpayee government in 1996? The Director CBI had lost his clout. My friend Shenoy [details in the CBI Insider Speaks (The Urea Scam)] spoke to L.K. Advani and, within a day, Indrajit Chowdhury received orders from the PMO to forward the concerned urea file. Two days later, the CBI Director had his orders. This was in May 1996. The Joint Director R. M. Singh, a CBI officer like me, was in overall charge of the investigation. He told me that when he zeroed in on Prabhakar Rao and other bureaucrats, not named in the FIR, Vijaya Rama Rao removed him to Chennai and handed over the investigation to an IPS officer on deputation to the CBI. Thereafter, the investigation did not proceed against either Prabhakar Rao or the bureaucrats, who had added National Fertilizer Corporation as an additional canalising agent, with the corrupt motive to buy urea – 200,000 metric tons for $ 38 million (₹133 crores). The regular buyer/canalising agent was the Minerals and Metals Trading Corporation (MMTC), a public sector under the Commerce Ministry and there was no complaint that its buying was causing a shortfall.

The new CBI Joint Director also sought my removal as a Consultant. That communication was shown to me by the new MD NFL, as the previous one was named as an accused by the CBI. Our complaint had not named him.

I exited. My six-month contract was thus truncated. But my good fairy was preparing a benediction.

The Commerce Secretary had opposed the NFL's entry in urea buying as the MMTC, under his Ministry, was fulfilling all current demands. He had also opposed the advance payment and kept a note of my strenuous attempt to rope all those guilty in this nefarious deal. In 1997, when he became Lt Governor of Delhi, he invited me to join his office as Special Secretary; to be his interface with Delhi Police. The Delhi Police reported to him directly. I had two tenures with him in the same capacity

1997-98 and 2007-2013. This was the benediction that I mentioned at the beginning of this account. During the 2007- 2013 tenure, when his boss, the Home Minister in my time in the CBI, the Minister of Internal Security and Minister of Personnel, wanted to oust me, suggesting that he employ a serving officer, instead of a retired officer like me, he evaded the issue and I continued to discharge my responsibilities. He also ignored the Delhi Chief Minister, Sheila Dikshit, in this regard. I regard this as a blessing.

Twenty-three years after the prosecution was launched by the CBI of those whom Vijay Rama Rao had chosen to prosecute, all the accused were convicted. The kickback proved was $4 million paid by the dubious Turkish company to the three Raos related to P.V. Narasimha Rao and even Prabhakar Rao, (not named accused) and to the son of Ram Lakhan Yadav (named an accused) then the Union Minister of Chemical and Fertiliser, when the NFL was made a canalising agent for importing urea in addition to the MMTC. Though the MD of the NFL and its Executive Director were convicted, there was no material to prove that they received any kickback. The bureaucrats, all Secretaries to Government, who compelled them to play a role in the NFL becoming a canalising agent, forcing them to make an advance payment of $38 million, were not touched.

Bully No. 5

Man from the megapolis

It was the month of May 1993. The venue was the North Block Committee room with the Minister of State for Home presiding. Among the participants were the Cabinet Secretary, some Home Ministry officials, the Director CBI and I. The subject for discussion was the March 1993 serial bomb blast in Mumbai, then known as Bombay. The investigation was with the Commissioner of Police, Bombay. From the CBI, I was regularly flying to Bombay and associating myself with the ongoing investigations. I was to take over the investigation in October 1993 when the Bombay police were to file a chargesheet. Thereafter, CBI was to investigate further and prosecute.

My association from early April with the ongoing Bombay Police investigations was ordered to ensure a seamless transfer of the case. Differences were already cropping up between us. I had questioned the prosecution of Sanjay Dutt as a terrorist. I also found little evidence to add to the 'Waging War' charge. That charge would apply, in my reckoning, if those prosecuted sought secession. I was told that the CM of Maharashtra wanted both. My saying no to both was disagreeable to those currently investigating the case.

At this meeting, the Cabinet Secretary, a Maharashtra cadre IAS said: "Sen travels every week for a few days to Bombay to join the 1993 blast investigations. Why not ask the CBI Joint Director in Bombay to replace Sen?" The Director CBI responded, "No. Never". The Cabinet Secretary, taken aback asked, "Why? What's wrong"? My Director, normally a mild person, retorted: "Everything is wrong". That put an end to the efforts of the megapolis bully to remove me at the outset. That was the first but not the last attempt.

I had no idea that CM Maharashtra was monitoring the case and he did not like my evidence-based views. Thus, it was equally true that I did not get my way. When they (Bombay police) filed the chargesheet in October 1993, they did obtain the sanction of the Government of India to add the 'Waging War' charge against all accused. My views were known but they were not considered even by the GOI. The CM Maharashtra prevailed. TADA was also applied to Sanjay Dutt. I still did not see the evidence.

The Special Public Prosecutor from CBI, appointed by the GOI at my recommendation was Mr Natarajan from Chennai. During my briefing, he independently came to the same conclusion as me. Legally, both of us were on sound footing. He told me that he would not argue to frame Waging of War (WoW) charges or terror charges against Sanjay Dutt in the trial court, as an independent prosecutor. He did so. The trial court did not frame waging of war charges. But he framed charges under TADA against Sanjay Dutt. However, the fat was in the fire and I was on the firing line.

When this argument was addressed in court, I was in Goa. Mr Natarajan had agreed not to argue that (WoW) charge would be dropped as a starting argument. He would drop the waging of war charges when he was winding up his argument on framing of charges against the accused. In Goa, I learnt, however, that his opening gambit was "I am dropping the Waging War charge "(WoW)." I had no time to personally inform either the Director or the Governments of India and Maharashtra in advance. When I asked Mr Natarajan why that opening gambit when we had agreed to do it at the end, his answer was unassailable. His sources had informed him that the opposite counsel, Majid Memon, had prepared himself only to contest the WOW charges and not on the other charges, conspiracy, TADA, murder or Arms Act or Explosive Substances Act and such others. So, if Natarajan dropped the WoW charge, Memon would have no ammunition to fire back. Other charges would not be contested. It happened almost as he anticipated.

When I reached Delhi from Goa I faced an upset Home Secretary, who was again an IAS officer from the Maharashtra cadre. His erstwhile boss, the CM Maharashtra had pulled him up. I told him the Special Public Prosecutor did not think the evidence to frame charges under section WoW was good and he told the court that he was dropping the charge as of now and would await better evidence from the investigators. I agreed with him. However, if the Government of India felt otherwise, we could sack him, engage a new Special

Prosecutor and instruct him to argue for framing charge on the section even though the evidence was palpably non-existent. That proposal had no buyers. Then I played my other card. I stated while the Special Public Prosecutor had acted within his powers, he was answerable to the Attorney General of India. We could refer his decision to drop this charge to the Attorney General. This opening was agreed to. Milon Kumar Banerji, our Attorney General examined his decision and concurred with the Special Public Prosecutor. That closed this chapter

But the CM Maharashtra was unhappy and the Bombay Police Joint Commissioner told me that he was going to fix me. Did he or did he not? I really do not know. What I do know is that I had a very bad last year in the CBI. The General Insurance Corporation (GIC), Chairman had, with the concurrence of the Secretary Insurance Government of India, sought to make me Managing Director (Vigilance GIC) once I retired but CVC, N. Vittal, scotched it by writing on the file: "I have reservations about Sen". The Chairman GIC, whose office is in Bombay, told me so himself. Was it somebody fixing me?

I might add that though the charges under TADA were framed against Sanjay Dutt he was convicted only under the Arms Act by the trial court and that decision of the trial court was maintained in the Supreme Court. Another cause of annoyance of those who wanted to see him convicted as a terrorist. The reason was that his father had annoyed the then M P when the latter contested for PM's chair in 1991 and SUNIL DUTT cast his vote in favour of P. V. Narasimha Rao, the only MP from Maharashtra to do so. This Sunil Dutt told me. Thus, when early on I agreed to his bail, which he got from the Supreme Court of CJI Ahmadi, I must have wounded armours. I also charged nine more, all Dawood men, who had not been investigated by the Commissioner of Police Bombay. There were 25 absconders, when they filed the first chargesheet. We arrested almost all of them. We improved the evidence considerably by filing, till April 1996, 16 more reports enhancing the evidence. Yet, politically, I found myself the odd one out throughout.

However, I had my way with this crossing of swords with a political bully.

THE END

Epilogue

I must add that till the near end, the CBI, as a department, stood behind me. When I returned from Sikkim, hurt and having resigned, two persons, J.S. Bawa. Director CBI, and E. Rennison, Joint Director helped me. Bawa rejected my resignation and Rennison sat down with me and bluntly said never to look for justice in the world. He assigned me an important branch and important investigations. My school companion, Kuldeep Mathur, had introduced me to T.N. Chaturvedi, the Home Secretary, whom he knew well. He gave me good advice 'when elephants fight, the grass only gets quashed' and protected my back from his underlings, who were too ready to carry on with Governor of Sikkim, Homi J.H. Taleyarkhan's animus against me. Later Directors, M.G. Katre, Rajendra Sekhar, S.K. Dutta, all IPS officers with stints in subordinate ranks in the CBI, before becoming Director also stood by me when political bullies were after my blood. Only my last Director, Vijay Rama Rao, who had no tenure in junior ranks in the CBI before becoming Director did not only not back me when I, as I thought, stood up for law, he harmed me. I strongly feel no one should be Director CBI without previous experience in the CBI. It is happening nowadays; it is a wrong practice and not a good thing for the CBI.

Speaking for myself with CBI-oriented Directors, I was never in any serious trouble. Later Tejendra Khanna always stood by me and till the age of 75 years, I was an important cog in the wheels of the Government here, the Government of Delhi.